Sociomaterial Practices in Medical Work

Attila Bruni

Sociomaterial Practices in Medical Work

An Ethnography in the Operating Room

Attila Bruni
Department of Sociology and Social Research
University of Trento
Trento, Italy

ISBN 978-3-031-44803-4   ISBN 978-3-031-44804-1   (eBook)
https://doi.org/10.1007/978-3-031-44804-1

Cover illustration: Pattern © Harvey Loake

This Palgrave Macmillan imprint is published by the registered company Springer Nature Switzerland AG.
The registered company address is: Gewerbestrasse 11, 6330 Cham, Switzerland

Paper in this product is recyclable.

ACKNOWLEDGMENTS

The ethnography presented in this book comes from the collaboration between the Research Unit on Communication, Organizational Learning, and Aesthetics (http://www.unitn.it/rucola) of the Department of Sociology and Social Research at the University of Trento and the Operational Unit of Occupational Medicine of the Trento Provincial Health Services Company (Azienda Provinciale per I Servizi Sanitari—APSS), within the project: "Safety, Culture, and Organizational Climate in the Operating Room," funded by the Cassa di Risparmio Foundation of Trento and Rovereto (CARITRO) and coordinated by Dr. Antonio Cristofolini of Trento APSS.

This book also has deep roots in the intellectual movement that today revolves around the debate on sociomateriality in organization, whose tradition could be traced back to studies on organizations as sociotechnical systems, and which has increasingly hybridized with contributions coming from other fields of study, primarily science and technology studies (STS).

The conception and writing of the text have benefited from discussions with various colleagues, and in particular: Francesco Bonifacio, Michela Cozza, Fabio Maria Esposito, Silvia Gherardi, Jannis Kallinikos, Paolo Magaudda, Francesco Miele, Davide Nicolini, Laura Lucia Parolin, Manuela Perrotta, Trevor Pinch, Cornelius Schubert, David Seibt, and Brit Ross Winthereik. The text has also benefited from feedback received during preliminary presentations of parts of the research at various sessions of the Egos Colloquium, EASST Conference, and STS-Italia

Conference. I would also like to thank Giusi Orabona for sharing the fieldwork and her fieldnotes with me. However, my deepest gratitude goes to the actors involved, without whose willingness, patience, and attention this research would not have been possible.

There are therefore numerous and well-articulated debts of gratitude, but the ultimate responsibility of this text lies solely with the author.

CONTENTS

LIST OF TABLES

CHAPTER 1

Introduction

Abstract This book originates from an ethnography of work in the operating room. Artifacts and technologies play a vital role in shaping work practices, and the book adopts a sociomaterial perspective to acknowledge the entanglements of social and material elements in surgical work and in organizational action. The introduction presents the main themes of the book and its outline.

Keywords Medical work • Sociomaterial practices • Ethnography • Organizational action

In the operating room, the radio is on and the clock reads 8:23 a.m.. Surrounding the operating table, on which a woman is already anesthetized, are three people: two surgeons (Dr. Pardo and Dr. Conti) and the instrument nurse (standing on a platform, to the patient's left). Dr. Pardo and Dr. Conti disinfect the surgical field. Meanwhile, the nurse anesthetist and anesthesiologist update each other about the patient's clinical condition. The operating field has been disinfected and at 8:41 a.m. everyone is at their "stations" ready to begin the surgery, a mastectomy.

Dr. Conti asks the room staff nurse to make a phone call. The room staff nurse reaches the preoperative area, picks up the phone and dials a number, but no one answers. After a while, he comes back and says, "Still nothing..."

A. Bruni, *Sociomaterial Practices in Medical Work*, https://doi.org/10.1007/978-3-031-44804-1_1

Instrument nurse: "But he must have told you something earlier, right?"
Room staff nurse: "Yes, that nobody answers at home and that the cell phone is unreachable."
Dr. Conti, since there is no news from Dr. Giglio (the surgeon who is to operate) and the surgery was supposed to start at 8:00 a.m. (it is now 8:50 a.m.), asks the room staff nurse to call in another surgeon (Dr. Sandri) as a replacement.

After a couple of minutes, Dr. Sandri enters the preoperative area, washes her hands, and after entering the operating room without greeting anyone, puts on gown, gloves, and protective mask and begins the surgery. While Dr. Sandri begins to incise the part to be operated on, the anesthesiologist checks the patient's physiological parameters through the monitor; the nurse anesthetist, next to her, finishes filling out the anesthesiology chart.

At 9:05 a.m., Dr. Giglio enters the operating room (without a mask and without returning the operators' greeting) and approaches Dr. Sandri. The latter, interrupting the surgery for a moment, turns and says to Dr. Giglio: "There seems to be no room for Ms. Vialli."

Dr. Giglio: "Move her!"
Dr. Sandri: "I've already moved her four times...."
Dr. Giglio: "Excuse me, but is she your sister?"
Dr. Sandri: "No...."
Dr. Giglio: "So what!?"

Dr. Giglio walks away to the sink (in the preroom) to wash his hands and returns to the room (this time with his mask on, although lowered under his nose). As she approaches the operating table, Dr. Sandri walks away and exits the room.

The aspirator is not working properly and there is a strong smell of burning, scorched skin. No one seems to be surprised and the instrument nurse asks the room staff nurse for water, which "takes away the burning smell," but the situation does not improve. The instrument nurse asks for more water, but this time the room staff nurse is intent on counting gauze, so the nurse anesthetist intervenes: "Leave it, I'll get it." The instrument nurse takes off her gloves (because they are particularly dirty), but she already has another pair underneath. Between the instrument nurse and Dr. Giglio, verbal exchanges are kept to a minimum, partly because the instrument nurse works in advance, not waiting for the surgeon to give her directions about the instruments she needs. The only verbal interactions occur between the instrument nurse and the room staff nurse (to check the gauze count) and between the *anesthesiologist and the nurse anesthetist (who discuss the patient's anesthesiology chart).*

Dr. Giglio tells the room staff nurse to take the prosthesis to be implanted (pointing to it with a number); the room staff nurse goes to a shelf on which there are about 20 boxes arranged on top of each other in five rows, takes one and hands it to the surgeon, who says: "Yes, this one." The three surgeons proceed with the surgery by inserting the prosthesis. Before the surgical field is closed, the instrument nurse gets off the platform placed next to the operating bed, walks to the foot of the bed, looks at the patient and says: "No, the right one is smaller." The anesthesiologist approaches the instrument nurse, looks at the patient and nods.

The prosthesis inserted is actually larger than it should be, so Dr. Giglio asks the room staff nurse for a smaller prosthesis while he proceeds to remove the first one. With the prosthesis replaced, Dr. Giglio, stepping away from the operating bed, says: "Good, you can close." He pulls off his gown and exits the room (again without saying goodbye), while the other two surgeons finish the surgery.

"Count!" says the instrument nurse to the room staff nurse, who replies: "20 plus 5."

Instrument nurse: "Okay, here we go."

Dr. Pardo 'closes' the patient, the room staff nurse takes away the bag containing the gauze used during the procedure, the instrument nurse cleans the patient of disinfectant and blood, and the nurse anesthetist takes the iron table to the sterilization room. The anesthesiologist, approaching the patient (who has since been extubated), says: "Come on, Anna, take nice deep breaths. It's all over, you know? Everything went well...." The patient meanwhile begins to gasp for breath. The anesthesiologist caresses the woman's face and continues to reassure her by telling her that it is all over. After a few minutes, the patient is already able to talk and to move from the operating bed to the gurney on her own, without anyone's help.

The episode just described marked the beginning of the ethnography from which this book originates. To be fair, the episode described preceded the actual fieldwork, having occurred at the beginning of a day of preliminary observation of work in the operating room, which was useful in getting an initial idea of the activity that was about to be observed.

Having no experience of work in the operating room, and given the anomalies that occur in the course of the episode (the delay in starting the procedure, the sloppy use of safety equipment, the apparent randomness that leads to the successful conclusion of the procedure), I thought I had witnessed an exceptional episode compared to the daily work routine of the place being observed. However, as the research continued, the episode began to appear more and more ordinary to me, until it became emblematic of working in that specific operating block and of the main working practices in the operating room *tout court*. Frequenting the operating block of just one hospital, I felt the need to document myself with respect to everyday working practices in other operating rooms and, fortunately, the literature offers numerous and diverse examples of research in this regard. Such readings helped me to better identify the peculiarities of the environment I observed, but also to relativize some of my impressions and interpretations, showing me how there was nothing 'strange' or 'special' about what I was observing.

But back to our episode: what is it emblematic of?

First, we can see how the work in the operating room is constructed as a continuous and uninterrupted flow. The different activities appear to follow one another in a fluid, almost "automatic" way (as for the synchrony of actions in the final phase of the surgery, once the gauze count is completed), as witnessed also by the fact that communications between operators are reduced to the essentials and always focused on specific aspects of the surgery in progress. The main expertise of the operators lies in working in anticipation, as in the case where the nurse anesthetist, seeing the room staff nurse intent on counting gauze, takes her place and hands water to the instrument nurse. Even the unforeseen events (the surgeon's tardiness; the vacuum cleaner not working properly; the wrong size of the prosthesis) seem to be immediately reabsorbed by what is the rhythm of daily work and the skill of the operators in improvising different solutions (finding another surgeon; using water to decrease the intensity of odors; changing perspective in observing the patient). Even a certain kind of variability in the use of personal protective equipments (the surgeon entering the room with the mask down) seems to be part of everyday work.

In secundis, however, the episode does not return a relaxed working atmosphere, mainly because of the delay with which the surgery begins and the abrupt ways in which the surgeons enter the scene and communicate with each other. Associated with this is the explicit violation of certain safety regulations (the operating room door remaining open; the surgeon's failure to wear personal safety equipment), the prolonged anesthesia to which the patient is subjected because of the delay in the start of the surgery, as well as the (wrong) size of the prosthesis that the surgeon implants at first. This is to say that no matter how smoothly the activities seem to flow, there are numerous elements that can engulf their progress and affect negatively actors' work and organizational practices.

Finally, it is important to emphasize the role played by technologies and technical objects. As the reported episode shows, work in the operating room is articulated not only through human action, but also through various technologies and tools, which constitute the material infrastructure on which everyday work practices rest. This is not to say that if a technology malfunctions, the work will necessarily grind to a halt: as in the case of the vacuum cleaner, actors are used at deploying alternative solutions to those envisioned, finding in the surrounding environment the resources useful for action. The issue thus lies in recognizing how the material world in which actors are immersed is not entirely inert, but rather continually interpellates them (as with the measurement of the prosthesis) and punctuates their time for action (as in the case of the gauze count, before the end of which the patient cannot be sutured). Objects and technologies "do" and "make do" (Akrich, 1992; Latour, 1992) and, in parallel, actors look at objects and technologies for allies to "do" and "make do" (Engeström & Blackler, 2005).

This last consideration is essential to the present research, as it constitutes one of its main theoretical-interpretive assumptions. As much as ethnographic orthodoxy would like the researcher to enter the field unencumbered by specific theoretical lenses (Silverman, 1997), my work has always been in the groove created between sociology of organization (OS) and science and technology studies (STS), with a particular attitude for actor-network theory (and its various articulations) and the idea that what we call "organization" (or "reality") is the result of a continuous heterogeneous engineering (Law, 1994), in an effort to hold together the different elements that organizing and working involve. This kind of theoretical sensibility now spills over into the concept of sociomateriality (Barad, 2003, 2007) and the idea that organizational and work practices are always, by definition, the result not of a sum of material and social elements, but of processes that are at the same time social *and* material. That is, that sociality and materiality are constantly and mutually implicated in (and by) organizational action and that, indeed, part of that action is aimed precisely at distinguishing and separating what should be considered as a whole. In other words, organizations are framed as sociomaterial assemblages.

As with any vivid debate, not all participants would agree with this kind of statement. Indeed, it could be argued that sociality and materiality are ontologically distinct, and only in practice, they become imbricated in each other (Leonardi, 2013). From such a perspective, organizational practices are precisely what fuse different elements (the social and the material) into a whole (sociomateriality).

These different accents and interpretations lead in the current debate to intellectual controversies that seem to undermine the validity and heuristic appropriateness of the concept of sociomateriality itself. In the face of the enormous body of theoretical literature that has developed around the concept of sociomateriality (Carlile et al., 2013; Hui et al., 2016; Leonardi et al., 2012), the aim of this book is to operationalize this concept from an ethnographic perspective. This means, on the one hand, to research and describe how sociomateriality emerges and takes shape in organizational and work practices. On the other, to show how a sociomaterial perspective allows and stimulates complex and original interpretations of organizational dynamics, at least in relation to work and organizing in the operating room (being the latter the empirical reference of this book).

1.1   Outline of the Book

What is the work in the operating room made of?

The first chapter provides an overview of the sociological and organizational literature on medical work, highlighting the mingling of human activities, technological artifacts, and organizational routines on which it is based. Then, the discourse turns to the concept of sociomateriality and to sociomaterial practices, referring in particular to the debate that has arose around these themes in the fields of organization studies (OS) and science and technology studies (STS). In particular, here I recall what could be considered the main theoretical impulses from which the concept of sociomateriality took its cue, acknowledging two compelling interpretations of the concept and addressing a possible solution in the idea of approaching sociomateriality in terms of 'degrees' (Cooren, 2020). After having outlined the distinctive contribution of STS-oriented investigations of the medical field, the chapter concludes by summarizing and eliciting the main theoretical characteristics of a sociomaterial approach to medical work.

Chapter 2 presents the methodology and the empirical research context. In particular, the chapter focuses on organizational ethnography, illustrating in theory and in practice its typical stages (accessing the field, fieldworking, interpreting data, leaving the field, and writing the final research report). The empirical context is represented by the operating block of a hospital located in a medium-sized province of the north-east of Italy. In order to observe everyday work, different actors of the operating block were shadowed (on a weekly basis), namely: one room staff nurse; one anesthetist nurse; one instrument assistant; one anesthesiologist; one surgeon; one entering instrument nurse; the instrument Head nurse; the operating theatre Head nurse. Independently of the operator observed, the shadowing activity located the observations within the same organizational space (the operating unit with its various rooms). This yielded ethnographic accounts that conveyed both the various work practices and professional visions to which actors might refer, and the specificity of the climate and the interactions that developed in the setting observed. But most of all, observations highlight the sociomaterial side of everyday work; that is, the ways in which objects and technologies participate in organizational processes and work practices while being performed by these same processes and practices.

In Chap. 3, the ethnography begins. Description and analysis focus on the ways in which organizational and work practices 'materialize' through different instruments, objects, and technologies. By means of various ethnographic episodes, the array of technologies and technical objects within an operating unit (e.g., personal safety devices, sanitary equipment, and machinery for the monitoring and life support of patients) is presented, showing their essential role in the performance of everyday activities. From an interpretative point of view, the chapter proposes the metaphor of 'flirtation' as a way to catch one of the main characteristics of everyday work in the operating room. That is, the intimate relationship, but never with entirely predictable outcomes, that arises between actors and the different materials they have to relate to in order to perform work and organizational practices. Finally, the chapter makes a point regarding the presence and the use of two mundane technologies commonly present into the operating room and which served as a background (or better, a sound track) to the flow of activities: the radio and the smartphone. Referring to various ethnographic excerpts, it will be shown how technologies pertaining to the mundane experience of the actors are 'put to work' and, at the same time, might interfere with other objects and practices.

But organizational and work practices 'materialize' also thanks to communicative acts; and communicative acts are essential to perform objects and technologies as well. How do objects and technologies participate in processes and practices of organizational communication? And in which ways communicative practices perform objects and technologies in work practices? These two questions underlie the fourth chapter, in order to further drawing attention on the sociomaterial side of medical work (and organizational action at large). Communicative practices, the way organizational communication is managed, and the materials implied in (and by) communicating play a central role in the operating room. Through a variety of ethnographic episodes, the chapter shows how objects and technologies are not just being talked about by humans, but they concretely intervene in actions and conversations. In relation to the communicative practices and the jargon which characterizes everyday interactions in the operating room, also the use of gender stereotypes will emerge, giving the occasion to reflect on the gender dimension of sociomaterial practices and medical work.

Chapter 5 focuses on the different professional expertise entailed by the activity in the operating room, but also on the knowledge that operators assume their colleagues have and that different professional communities attribute to each other. The fieldnotes' interpretation will show not only the multiple professional visions that guide the evaluations and the decisions of organizational actors, but also the role objects and technologies have in the making and in the performance of professional knowledge. In particular, the chapter highlights the "material awareness" and the "symbiotic materialism" which allow actors to perform and adapt plans to situated action. As we will see, also power materializes in the relationships between different professionals and communities of practice, sometimes through the use of technical objects and other material artifacts.

In the Conclusions, I offer some reflections regarding the articulation of work and organizational practices in the operating room, arguing that although social and material aspects are inherently entangled, the extent and consequences of this entanglement can vary. Therefore, a closer look into sociomaterial entanglements is needed to question their matter and organizational implications.

REFERENCES

Akrich, M. (1992). The De-scription of Technical Objects. In Bijker, W. & Law, & J. (eds.), *Shaping Technology/Building Society. Studies in Sociotechnical Change* (pp. 205–224). Cambridge, MA, MIT Press.

Barad, K. (2003). Posthumanist Performativity: Toward an Understanding of How Matter Comes to Matter. *Signs, 28*(3), 801–831.

Barad, K. (2007). *Meeting the Universe Halfway: Quantum Physics and the Entanglement of Matter and Meaning.* Duke University Press.

Carlile, P. R., Nicolini, D., Langley, A., & Tsoukas, H. (Eds.). (2013). *How Matter Matters: Objects, Artifacts, and Materiality in Organization Studies* (Vol. 3). Oxford University Press.

Cooren, F. (2020). Beyond Entanglement: (Socio-) Materiality and Organization Studies. *Organization Theory, 1*, 1–24.

Engeström, Y., & Blackler, F. (2005). On the Life of the Object. *Organization, 12*, 307–330.

Hui, S., Shove, E., & Schatzki, T. (Eds.). (2016). *The Nexus of Practices: Connections, Constellations, and Practitioners.* Routledge.

Law, J. (1994). *Organizing Modernity.* Blackwell.

Latour, B. (1992). Where are the missing masses, sociology of a few mundane artefacts. In W. Bijker and J. Law (eds) *Shaping Technology-Building Society. Studies in Sociotechnical Change*, Cambridge, MA, MIT Press, pp. 225–259.

Leonardi, P. M. (2013). Theoretical Foundations for the Study of Sociomateriality. *Information and Organization, 23*(2), 59–76.

Leonardi, P. M., Nardi, B. A., & Kallinikos, J. (Eds.). (2012). *Materiality and Organizing: Social Interaction in a Technological World.* Oxford University Press.

Silverman, D. (1997). *Doing Qualitative Research.* Sage.

CHAPTER 2

Medical Work and Sociomaterial Practices: A Theoretical Overview

Abstract This chapter provides an overview of the sociological and organizational literature on medical work, highlighting the mingling of human activities, technological artifacts, and organizational routines on which it is based. Then, the discourse turns to the concept of sociomateriality and to sociomaterial practices, referring in particular to the debate that arose around these themes in the fields of organization studies and STS. The chapter concludes by summarizing and eliciting the main theoretical characteristics of a sociomaterial approach to medical work.

Keywords Medical work • Organization studies • Science and technology studies • Sociomaterial practices

> *"Theory is overwritten, we got more theory than we can possibly use."*
> *(John Van Maanen, 12/7/2020—meeting in honour of Barbara Czarniawska)*

2.1 MEDICAL WORK: BODIES, ARTIFACTS, AND ROUTINES

What does medical work consist of? What is it 'made of'?

Being a sociologist, the first answer that comes to mind is from my discipline. Sociology is used to trace back to Parsons (1951) the first

© The Author(s), under exclusive license to Springer Nature Switzerland AG 2023
A. Bruni, *Sociomaterial Practices in Medical Work*,
https://doi.org/10.1007/978-3-031-44804-1_2

manifestation of explicit interest in medicine. He identified the medical profession as the main agency for controlling the destructive nature of disease by virtue of a medical knowledge characterized by affective neutrality and universality. In Parsonsian sociology, illness is framed as an unnatural state of the human body, potentially causing physical and social dysfunction (Turner, 1987). Therefore, the medical profession becomes the primary agency for controlling the destructive nature of illness, and medical knowledge is characterized by affective neutrality and universality. The doctor-patient relationship is naturally harmonious and consensual, albeit marked by an inherent power asymmetry.

Because of its localization of disease within the biological functions of the body, the functionalist-Parsonsian interpretation of medicine has been variously criticized over the years. One of the most radical critiques emerged in the 1970s by Marxist sociology, which interprets medicine as an institution of control acting consistently with the economic-political interests of capitalist society (Freidson, 1970; Illich, 1976). From this perspective, the capitalist system promotes a view of health as a commodity (Epstein, 1978), in which the pursuit of profit is one of the most influential factors. However much a Marxist perspective leads to different conclusions from those expressed by the functionalist current, it does not introduce new analytical elements: medical work is studied in structural terms, on the basis of the 'function' it performs (or should perform) in a given social system.

The poststructuralist tradition, in accordance with Foucault's (1963) genealogical approach, considers medical knowledge and practice not as independent of social reality, but actively involved in the construction of that reality. To the mind/body distinction assumed by functionalist views is preferred the notion of embodiment (Turner, 1992) and a framing of medicine as an expression of specific historical, cultural, political, and economic processes.

Alongside these three traditions, there is finally a fourth one in sociology, inspired by a phenomenological and interactionist view, and which has given rise to a number of ethnographies of medical work that today represent classics not only for those involved in the study of medicine and healthcare. Just think of *Asylum*, by Erving Goffman (1961), based on ethnographic research inside a large psychiatric hospital of the United States. Here, Goffman, describing the roles and lived experiences of hospital workers and patients, introduces (among others) the concept of "total institution" to describe those organizations separated from the outside world (such as psychiatric hospitals, but also prisons, schools, or monasteries) and in which residents are deprived of their previous social identities and subject only to the rules of the organization. Such a concept is now part of the theoretical apparatus of the entire social sciences, and the echo of *Asylum* bypassed the boundaries of sociology and made it an essential reference also for the development of a critical perspective toward long-term psychiatric asylums.

Another ethnography that had considerable resonance was the one conducted a few years later by David Sudnow (1967) inside two U.S. hospitals. Here, the author highlighted how hospitals are not just places of care, but complex organizational contexts, within which practices, roles, and interactions guided by partly different logics take shape and where a range of social inequalities are reproduced. Sudnow dwelt in particular on what he labeled as "social death":

> i.e., where death is the warrantable basis for doing such things as planning an autopsy, disposing of personal effects, contracting mortuary institutions, putting a body in the morgue, informing insurance companies (…), and, generally, engaging in those organizational, ceremonial, and economic activities associated with death, those matters which mark the end of social existence. (Sudnow 1967, p. 75)

The "social death" thus refer to the set of actions that hospital staff take when the patient is not biologically dead but is deemed moribund. The care administered becomes palliative in nature, and a series of actions that anticipate the patient's death begin to take place: the ward chaplain (who will give last rites) is informed, and it may be that a nurse closes the patient's eyes, because the eyelids are still elastic (following death, the muscles stiffen and the eyelids become less mobile), but also because it is socially desired that the body of a deceased person resembles that of a sleeping person (Sudnow, 1967). After the biological death (which in a hospital ward is a relatively ordinary event), the staff then undertakes a series of actions aimed at satisfying certain organizational issues: the door to the room is closed, the nurse talks to the deceased's family members, the corpse is covered with a sheet, hands and feet are tied with special ribbons bearing a label for future recognition. But it is not necessarily the case, Sudnow (1967) notes, that social death and biological death always follow one another in the same order: there are cases in which social death follows biological death, which is purposely not detected by hospital staff in order to shift a number of unpleasant tasks, such as having to attend to the patient's cosmetics, onto colleagues. Just as often the social status of patients becomes one of the criteria that directs the attention of hospital staff, and can anticipate or delay the activation of the dying process.

Sudnow's research thus highlighted how hospital activity unfolds through a series of practices, ritual interactions, and work routines that bring attention back to the organizational dimension of what a few years later Glaser and Strauss (1965), in the context of another research on the terminally ill, defined as the "trajectory of death." This reference to the organizational dimension of medical work was already present in another well-known ethnography of the time, *Boys in Whyte* (Becker et al., 1961), a study of the learning trajectory of medical students. Becker and colleagues were indeed highlighting how the study of medicine requires the learning of rules, values, knowledge, and practices that obey to criteria internal to the medical profession, thus giving rise to a specific professional and organizational culture.

But the text that probably best captures the organizational dimension of medical work is *The Social Organization of Medical Work* (Strauss et al., 1985). Here, the concept of "disease trajectory" is employed to refer "not only to the physiological resolution of the patient's illness, but to the entire organization of the work performed during the course of the illness, together with the impact (of the trajectory) on the people involved in that work and its organization" (Strauss et al., 1985, 8; emphasis in original).

Strauss et al. (1985) identify five main areas in which organizational and work processes associated with managing an illness trajectory are mainly expressed:

1. Work related to the maintenance and use of technology and machinery (machine work);
2. work related to ensuring the safety of patients and operators (safety work);
3. work directed toward patients in order to alleviate their most immediate physical suffering (comfort work);
4. work necessary for the performance of standardized care tasks but requiring individualized attention as they are directed toward living, sentient and responsive subjects (sentimental work);
5. work useful in establishing, maintaining, and changing the arrangements necessary to complete a task and/or what was previously planned (articulation work).

For the purposes of our discussion, it may be particularly useful to dwell on what perhaps not coincidentally Strauss and colleagues identify as the first type of work, machine work.

Entering a hospital, they write, one immediately notices a variety of machines and technologies (Strauss et al., 1985). These are essential to the proper performance of daily work and are constitutive of medical practice itself, as in reference to procedures that would otherwise be impossible to perform (as in the case of an X-ray or an operation under anesthesia), as in relation to more everyday activities. Consider, for example, ordinary technology such as inpatient beds (Strauss et al., 1985: 102). Initially, the beds were "fixed," and helping a nonautonomous patient change position was part of the comfort work of the nurses, who in this way also ensured that the patient assumed a correct posture in relation to his or her condition. As a result of bed mechanization, patients can change position simply by pressing a few buttons, but this is not enough to ensure their comfort. In fact, now the clinical staff care less about the patient's own posture, whose comfort is thus exposed to new problems resulting from the nurses' reduced attention to the position assumed.

This example illustrates the close relationship that ties nursing practices, work and organizational routines, technologies and the articulation of activities, as well as how the use of a new machinery/technology always involves a shift traditional trajectories of action (Strauss et al., 1985). This is because the use of technological artifacts and technical objects, especially if they are 'new,' confronts actors and the organization with problems that were unexpected or unknown until the time of the introduction of such artifacts. As an example, we can recall what has happened as a result of the massive entry of information and communication technologies (ICT) into hospitals and care processes. Such technologies have enabled the digitization of clinical data and, consequently, the creation of a whole range of new systems for managing and sharing such data. Thus, various devices and software have appeared for remote monitoring of chronic patients (as in the case of telecardiology services aimed at heart failure patients); teleconsultation systems (i.e., the ability for two or more differently located healthcare professionals to share and discuss data, images, and information about patients in real time); devices for self-monitoring by patients (as in the case of blood glucose devices in diabetic patients); and, more recently, the so-called self-tracking and wearable technologies that monitor and record certain vital parameters (such as blood pressure or heart rate). Not only that, on a par with most organizations, ICTs have also made their entry into common organizational processes, in the form of electronic patient records, software for managing and storing clinical data, and programs to support the setting of treatment plans or automated drug distribution.

Since the 1990s, medical practice becomes a privileged empirical reference for observing the relationships that reciprocally link human actors, technological artifacts, scientific knowledge, and everyday work practices (Casper & Berg, 1995). Focusing on the role of diverse tools (software, guidelines, protocols) in the 'rationalization' of medical work, Berg (1997) shows how different technologies embody different configurations of what 'medical practice' is, what 'science' is, and what constitutes a 'rational' medical knowledge. Medical practice and instruments reciprocally construct each other: the development of instruments is inextricably bound up with the emergence of (and competition from) new forms of medical rationality, just as a new instrument establishes the boundaries between what is 'rational' and medical practice itself. To summarize, protocols, clinical guidelines, and decision-support technologies are the means by which medical knowledge and its practice are rationalized (Berg et al., 2000; Moreira, 2005). The initial study of 'medical practice as technology' (Casper & Berg, 1995) evolves over the years into study of the 'practice of medical technology' (Timmermans & Berg, 2003), thereby further demonstrating that medicine has acquired the features of a technology in itself (Elston, 1997).

Hospital environments thus become an ideal space to observe the mingling of human bodies and technological equipment, mundane and scientific knowledge, local actions, and global standards (Timmermans & Berg, 2003, 2004). Everyday and futuristic technologies, drugs, organizational devices, and infrastructures are all embedded in a network of actions and interactions, the assemblage of which, however, is always precarious and susceptible to change when in relation to other tools, practices, groups of actors, and professional knowledges (Bruni, 2008).

Given these premises, one can see how hospitals represent today the crossroads of various technologies and technologically mediated relationships, offering a privileged field of observation for the study of how (new) technologies become part of organizational processes and work practices. Moreover, in contemporary hospitals, one finds pens and computers, paper and digital files, post-it notes, and e-mails. Some of these tools appear newer than others, but this does not detract from the fact that a pen and a computer are both technologies and that one of the possible difficulties lies precisely in having to use them within the same activity (Bruni, 2015). This highlights another issue regarding technologies in hospital organizations, that is, their layering, rather than their harmonious replacement or succession. Not coincidentally, several researches show that the difficulties associated with the use of new technological objects (an electronic patient record, or a device for recording and transmitting electrocardiographic traces) may arise not so much from the intrinsic characteristics of the technology itself, but from having to align the use of these technologies with other tools and activities already present in the organization (Bruni, 2005; Bruni & Rizzi, 2013).

2.2   SOCIOMATERIALITY: WHERE DOES IT COME FROM?

"Sociomateriality is the new Black," wrote Jarzabrowski and Pinch already in 2013. In 2016, a page was created on Wikipedia defining sociomateriality: *"a theory built upon the intersection of technology, work and organization, that attempts to understand"* the constitutive entanglement of the social and the material in everyday organizational life. *"It is the result of considering how human bodies, spatial arrangements, physical objects, and technologies are entangled with language, interaction, and practices in organizing."*

This is to say that the concept of sociomateriality does not represent a novelty nowadays and that, although adopted in different fields of the social sciences and with reference to different objects of study, one of its main fields of application is that of studies developed at the intersection of STS and OS. This intersection has developed since the 1980s thanks to a series of studies questioning the conventional distinctions between the social and the material and, above all, emphasizing the continuous cross-references between the social character of technologies and objects and the materiality of social and organizational processes (Callon, 1986; Latour, 1992; Pickering, 1995; Knorr Cetina, 1997; Law, 1992). The distinction between social and material, in this perspective, is only analytical, so that Law and Mol already in 1995 wrote:

Perhaps materiality and sociality are produced together. Perhaps the association is not only about human beings, but also about the material. Perhaps, then, when we look at the social, we look at the same time at the production of materiality. And when we look at materials, perhaps we are also looking at sociality. (Law & Mol, 1995, 1)

Actor-network theory and postfeminist studies are usually quoted as the main sources of inspiration for a sociomaterial approach (Orlikowski, 2007; Orlikowski & Scott, 2008). In particular, and without any claim of exhaustiveness, I would like to recall five concepts that from my point of view effectively summarize the theoretical impulses from which the concept of sociomateriality takes its cue: heterogeneous engineering; relational materialism; script and affordances; material-semiotic. Some of them may sound obvious to expert researchers, but in a sociological vein, this is not enough to simply taking them for granted. On the contrary, recalling them is a way to affirm their meaning, relevance, and utility. Paraphrasing Law (2001), it can indeed be said that like objects, concepts also interpellate us.

The first concept that forms the background of a sociomaterial approach is that of heterogeneous engineering (Law, 1987). That is, the process that makes the organization of people, texts, technologies, and objects (relatively) stable in time and space. According to Law (1994: 2), "what we call 'the social' is materially heterogeneous: discourses, bodies, texts, machines, architectures-all these elements and many others are implicated in the social and its performance." This leads to a symmetrical view of reality: all 'materials' contribute to making sense of social ordering, while as they themselves are the product (or effect) of an ordering work. subjectivity itself is the effect of a network of heterogeneous materials, an ordering process that is categorized as 'person':

> People are networks. Each of us constitutes a more or less stable positioning of elements. We are organisms insofar as we are sets of skin, bones, enzymes, cells and other elements over which we have no control and about which we share approximate knowledge. And if we are people instead of organisms, it is because we manage to hold together additional 'pieces': clothes, machines and other 'properties' that are only occasionally under our control (Law, 1994, 33).

Among the many studies that have shown how organizational activity can be interpreted as a process of heterogeneous engineering, the one conducted by Lucy Suchman (2000) about activities related to bridge design shows how the activity of organizing requires the constant alignment (Latour, 1990) of various forms of action and of different elements (technical, social, political, legal). Indeed, Suchman (2000, 323) shows how in the controversies and problems that dot the construction of the bridge there are at least two different artifacts in question: the bridge 'of the engineers' and that 'of the citizens.' Each of the two is underpinned by different networks-of-action, which thus lead to differential consideration of the choices and constraints involved in the construction of the bridge. The bridge 'of the engineers' takes shape through a project that in turn includes precise timelines and professional practices; the bridge 'of the citizens' includes different elements that refer back to the daily lives of those who live and move in a given area.

The concept of heterogeneous engineering is thus intended to emphasize how the work of building a new technological artifact is, to a significant extent, also a matter of organizing and, conversely, how organizational processes include the alignment of numerous tangible and intangible artifacts. "The sustainable reproduction of such enduring alignments, through processes of organization as much as construction, is the stuff of which bridges are made of," Suchman (2000, 325) concludes.

The second concept, closely related to the previous one, is that of relational materialism. If the social is the result of a heterogeneous engineering, then it is necessary to consider the different materials involved (texts, bodies, technologies, architectures, animals), not forgiving that "materials are better treated as products or effects rather than as having properties that are given in the order of things" (Law, 1994, 24). This means focusing on the relationships between different elements, rather than on the elements themselves, since it is in the mutual relationships that these elements acquire meaning and identity. Relational materialism is thus a processual ontology, which finds in the symmetry of relations its pivotal principle. This implies that even abstract entities like power, love, capitalism, or care are materially embodied in the relations between various elements (cultural, technical, textual) and that these relations can be observed empirically. Materiality and sociality are thus the joint effect of various organizational strategies (Law & Mol, 1995), humans and nonhumans are the alternate product of social and technical relations (Latour, 2002), and stability lies in the possibility of shaping the heterogeneity of the social.

Not all relations are equal, however. "Certain material, or combinations of material, effects are more durable, or more easily transported, than naked human bodies or their voices alone" (Law, 1994). The concept of relational materialism is thus also meant to draw attention to the unequal effects that relationships and materials generate and thus to the fact that any attempt at ordering is precarious and, just as it generates standards, it inevitably generates exceptions and inequalities (Star, 1996). Hence, the idea of ordering and organizing as never ending processes.

Then, there is the concept of script (Akrich, 1992), which is essential for approaching objects and technologies as active rather than inert elements. The script refers to what is inscribed into an object in the design process and that, as in a choreography, outlines roles, skills, and possibilities for action for those who interact with that artifact. In other words, the script prescribes the skills and the actions necessary for an artifact to function in the manner and for the purposes envisioned by its designers. Objects then not only "do" (in the sense that they embody human action, as in the case of a key, hinge, or door opener—Latour, 1992), but "make do," since they require humans to act in particular ways (otherwise, the object could not function properly, or break down, as commonly written in instruction manuals).

In order to build a useful vocabulary to account for the relational yet material nature of objects, it is then useful to counterbalance the concept of script with that of affordance (Gibson, 1979). Technologies, objects, and more generally the material world around us not only place constraints on action, but also offer a range of opportunities, invitations, and occasions. A knife has the affordance of cutting, threatening, or opening a window hook; a path offers the walker an affordance of locomotion from one place to another; water gives the affordance of wetting, washing, or pouring; fire gives an affordance of heat, but also of injury and light; and so on. The fact that the material world posits different affordances means, therefore, that natural and technical elements can acquire different identities depending on the activity that constructs them on a practical level, but always from certain material factors (Harré, 2002). In this sense, it is important to note how affordances draw actors' attention to some of the possibilities offered by the environment (a door 'invites' passage), but at the same time depend on actors' interests and capacity for action (actors do not necessarily seek the affordance of passage, nor is the opening of the door immediately accessible to everyone). Objects are constructed in the relations that they establish with humans and with other objects, and their performance of a more or less active role in social life is due not to their properties but to the type of relation they perform.

If, therefore, the concept of script draws attention to the more 'prescriptive' aspects of objects (emphasizing what users are required to knowing or doing to properly relate with an object or technology), that of affordance allows to thematize the different uses and actions to which the materiality of objects can invite, regardless of what the designers envisage and in relation to the actors' interests.

The last concept I propose as an illustrious antecedent of a sociomaterial approach is the one of material-semiotic. Like the other concepts presented, it was primarily meant to be an attempt to explore in unison the semiotic and material aspects of reality and the practices that constitute it (Law, 2007, 2019). Originally, material semiotics was sketched to investigate the making and the stabilization of scientific facts (Latour, 1988; Law, 2019) and to indicate the intertwinement of the natural and the cultural. Donna Haraway implied it in a peculiar way, defining bodies as "material-semiotic generative nodes" (Haraway, 1988: 22), and stressing how it is not possible to distinguish imaginary and material *a priori*, since they are realized together (as for the famous trope of the cyborg). If bodies are material-semiotic nodes, this implies that not only scientific knowledge, but any form of knowledge is always dependent on the conditions of its production and is always and everywhere embodied. Therefore, knowledge is not detached, but situated in particular bodies, technologies, networks of actors (human and nonhuman), and apparatuses of meaning production. Far from being a limitation, it is precisely in recognizing such situatedness ("a view from somewhere," as Haraway famously defined it) that lies the possibility of arriving at an 'objective' of knowledge.

By showing how "primates" or "patriarchy" are complex and not always coherent constructs, made up of heterogeneous practices, relations, and meanings, Haraway (1991) highlights how reality is plural (realities) not because of its different interpretations, but because it is differently actualized. The concept of material-semiotic thus reminds us that reality is multiple, and multiply realized, it is "done in practice" and practiced into being in heterogeneous networks of relations (Law, 2019). Material semiotics starts from the premise that reality is always situated and different-in-itself, and here lies the responsibility of practicing it.

2.3   SOCIOMATERIALITY IN ORGANIZATION: TWO COMPELLING VIEWS

The concept of sociomateriality is grafted into the conceptual landscape just described and found fertile ground in OS initially through the work of Wanda Orlikowski and her translation of Karen Barad's thought into the organizational debate (Orlikowski, 2007; Orlikowski & Scott, 2008). In an article that appeared in *Signs* a few years earlier, Barad (2003) referring to various strands of studies (feminism, poststructuralism, queer theory, Marxism, STS) asserted the need to overcome the linguistic turn (with its emphasis on meanings and representation) by paying attention to the materiality of action. Or rather, by looking for the mutual cross-references that come between the discursive and the material:

"materiality is discursive (...), just as discursive practices are always already material (...). The relationship between the material and the discursive is one of mutual entailment. Neither is articulated/articulable in the absence of the other; matter and meaning are mutually articulated. Neither discursive practices nor material phenomena are ontologically or epistemologically prior. Neither can be explained in terms of the other. Neither has privileged status in determining the other." (Barad, 2003, 822).

Three additional concepts are associated with the idea of the constitutive reciprocity of the material and the discursive: entanglement, intra-action, and agential realism. Although in the reported passage Barad speaks of "entailment," in his 2007 book, this word is replaced by "entanglement," in order to express the idea that the material-discursive is not the result of the union between two separate entities, but a unicum in which matter and discourse are mutually defined. Being inseparable, between matter and discourse, there is not interaction but intra-action (Barad, 2003). Thus, it is precisely through a specific form of intra-action, an agential cut, that "the boundaries and properties of the 'components' of phenomena become determinate and that particular embodied concepts become meaningful (...) effecting a separation between 'subject' and 'object'" (Barad, 2003, 815).

In order to problematize the boundaries between what are usually thought of as dichotomous elements, Barad proposes an "agential realist" standpoint:

"an epistemological-ontological-ethical framework that provides an understanding of the role of human and nonhuman, material and discursive, and natural and cultural factors in scientific and other social-material practices." (Barad, 2007, 26)

Here, we come to "social-material practices," an expression Barad uses only twice in *Meeting the Universe Halfway* and essentially interchangeably with "material-social" (three times) and, more importantly, with the one she favors: "material-discursive" (Barad, 2003, 2007).

A few years later, Orlikowski (2007) refers to sociomateriality as an "umbrella term" in order to cover the various contributions and strands of studies that since the scallops of Michel Callon (1986) and actor-network theory (Latour, 1988) tried to promote a relational and symmetric understanding of organizational processes. The absence of the hyphen between the "socio" and the "material" should stress precisely the constitutive entanglement of the two, in contrast to other research approaches (such as technological determinism or social construction of technology) which frame them as separate entities.

Orlikowski (2007) has been particularly effective in tracing the characteristics of a sociomaterial approach, and her work is so widely quoted (3875 quotations on Google scholar at mid-2023) that I will not repeat her arguments. I would simply recall the five main 'claims' of sociomateriality (Jones, 2014):

1. materiality is central to the understanding of contemporary organizations;
2. the social and the material are inextricably entangled;
3. entities are relational and do not have inherent properties;
4. boundaries between the social and material are enacted, not given;
5. practices matter, not cognition.

Already in 2014 Matthew Jones traced a brilliant account of the term "sociomateriality" and of its adoption in OS and IS, identifying two major understandings of the concept, a "weak" and a "strong" one (see Table 2.1).

The main difference between the two versions lies in their ontological assumptions. A 'strong' version assumes that everything *is* sociomaterial and that the separation between the social and the material is the effect of various (sociomaterial) practices. A 'weak' one takes the social and the material as ontologically different but in a relation of interdependency, so that they become *imbricated* in practice (Leonardi, 2013).

Leonardi (2013), in particular, has argued that these two different understandings of the concept of sociomateriality have serious implications in terms of potential conceptual contribution to OS. In his view, to start from the premise that the social and the material are entangled tends to produce a tautological effect. That is: "to demonstrate that organizing occurs in practice and that practice is neither social nor material; it is both" (Leonardi, 2013, 74). On the contrary, to look at the social and the material as imbricated (but still distinct) entities allows to seriously question how organizations and technologies mingle with each other, moving "technology into a constitutive role in organizing and organizational processes while showing how organizing shapes technology" (Leonardi, 2013, 74).

Table 2.1 Comparison between different interpretations of the concept of sociomateriality (adapted from Jones, 2014, p. 920)

Strong and weak sociomateriality compared

	Materiality	Inseparability	Performativity	Relationality	Practices
Strong (Barad, 2003, 2007; Orlikowski, 2007)	Materialization of phenomena	Mutual constitution	Enactment of boundaries and relations	Form, attributes, and capabilities of entities emerge only through interpenetration	Embodied, materially mediated arrays of human activity
Weak (Leonardi, 2012, 2013)	Persistence of arrangement of materials across place and time	Mutual interdependency	Nonhuman agency	Form, attributes, and capabilities may preexist any relation	Activities and processes

Beyond determining which of these two positions is 'stronger' (strength and weakness are also relational), one of the effects produced by the disagreement between the entanglement and imbrication metaphors has been to have shifted the debate to a theoretical dimension that, while rich in insights (Carlile et al., 2013; Hui et al., 2016), perhaps does not help to operationalize the concept from an empirical perspective.

Among various contributions, Francois Cooren (2020) has argued how the interest of a sociomaterial approach lies in looking at organizational phenomena from a processual and relational perspective. The focus of the analysis is thus on the materialization of organizational relationships, bearing in mind that: "this materialization does not consist of transforming something completely immaterial into something material, but of passing from one matter to another" (Cooren, 2020, 2). In this way, sociomateriality becomes a question of degrees:

> "The terms 'social' and 'material' are, in fact, adjectives and as such refer to the properties of everything that exists, whether we are talking about a technology, a rock, a human being, an emotion, a discourse, an organization, or a society" (Cooren, 2020, 14).

According to the author, both the entanglement and the imbrication metaphor tend to be misleading, as they both reproduce the idea of the social and the material as elements that however strongly "twisted, wrapped or woven together (...) can still be, at least theoretically, identified separately" (Cooren, 2020: 14). It is no coincidence that several sociomaterially oriented studies continue to associate the 'material' with what can be seen or touched (objects, technologies, architectures) and the 'social' with what is not physically present (thoughts, discourses, meanings), thus perpetuating the distinction between social and material that the sociomaterial approach would like to challenge.

In Cooren's view, in order to see sociomateriality in terms of 'properties' and 'degrees,' we need to understand it communicatively, "as studying communication implies, by definition, that we pay attention to *what links or relates beings to each other*" (Cooren, 2020: 2, italics in original). Here, Cooren's argumentation nicely echoes the attention early actor-network theory devoted to 'intermediaries' (whatever circulates between actors and defines their relationships—Callon, 1991). The distinction between the social and the material is thus not particularly apt in that, for example: "Communication, in order to occur, always needs to materialize into something or someone" (Cooren, 2020, 2).

Effectively systematizing the debate on sociomateriality and dispelling some of its theoretical knots in OS, Cooren generates a discursive approach to sociomateriality (exemplified by the CCO perspective *à la* Montreal). This juxtaposes with the two approaches traditionally referred to Orlikowski and Leonardi and, in its emphasis on the constitutive role of communicative processes for the materialization of organizational dynamics, it represents a further thread to follow in articulating the concept of sociomateriality in OS.

2.4   SOCIOMATERIALITY IN MEDICAL PRACTICE: THE CONTRIBUTION OF STS

As I have argued, the concept of sociomateriality has illustrious predecessors in the STS debate, but it has found a specific field of application in OS (and IS), giving rise to a debate that has led to different interpretations of the concept.

Orlikowski (2007) writes that she borrows the term "sociomateriality" from the work of Annemarie Mol (2002), and Lucy Suchman (2007), especially when the latter defines the configuration of users and machines (and, more generally, of reality) as a "sociomaterial assemblage." To be even more precise, Suchman adopts the expression "sociomaterial" already in a 2002 article on "situated accountabilities." Perhaps even more than in *Human-Machine Reconfigurations*, here she emphasizes the relevance of feminist studies of science and technology for the development of alternative practices of technology production, use, and for an overall reconstruction of the idea of objectivity. The core of her argument is that working relations are: "sociomaterial connections that sustain the visible and invisible work required to construct coherent technologies and put them into use" (Suchman, 2002: 91). Thus, there is a great responsibility in the way such technologies and their sociomaterial connections are represented, figured, and performed.

In both her article and her book, Suchman (2002, 2007) does not provide an analytical definition of "sociomaterial" or "sociomateriality." As it is typical in STS and feminist studies (Mol et al., 2010; Law, 2009), the definition of the concept is not articulated through formal and abstract propositions, but through reference to case studies, research, and firsthand lived experience. Among the many references made by Suchman, one is of particular interest to our discussion. In the concluding chapter ("Reconfigurations"), Suchman devotes space to several STS studies conducted in the context of medical work. The choreography of medical practitioners, machines, and practices through which patients in surgery are "transitioned" through anesthetic states

(Goodwin, 1994); the assemblage of bodies, technologies, knowledges, scientific, and medical practices through which fertility and pregnancy are produced (Cussins, 1998; Thompson, 2005); the societal and technological practices through which "fetal patient" are actualized (Casper, 1994, 1998); the work nurses and technicians perform in order to align the technologically dense environment of an operating room (Aanestad, 2003); in Suchman's view, these are all telling inquiries of a sociomaterial approach which leads to look at agency as "an effect of practices that are multiply distributed and contingently enacted" (Suchman, 2007: 267).

In my intellectual biography, indeed, the concept of sociomateriality is primarily linked to STS studies of medicine and, in particular, to Annemarie Mol's book *The Body Multiple*. At the very beginning of the book, Mol (2002: 6) writes: "ontology is not given in the order of things, (…) instead, ontologies are brought into being, sustained, or allowed to wither away in common, day-to-day, sociomaterial practices." As for Suchman, neither Mol offers an analytical definition of "sociomaterial" or "sociomateriality"; not only, the term basically disappears from the rest of the book, and it does not even appear in the analytical index.

At the same time, it would be easy to argue that (as from the above quotation) the entire book is about the sociomaterial entanglements that maintain medical practice and that in medical practice emerge. Just as an example, consider the following passage where Mol comments how atherosclerosis becomes visible "under a microscope," as a pathology resident once said to her:

> But it (the expression "under the microphone") implies a lot. Without this addition, atherosclerosis is all alone. It is visible *through* a microscope. A thickened intima. There is something seductive about it. To bow one's head over a microscope and let one's eyes be directed by the pointer. If only because a vessel cross section makes for a beautiful image. With all its pink and purple and its strange forms that slowly come to be discernible if their nature is explained. There's something seductive about it: to use instruments as "mere" instruments that unveil the hidden reality of atherosclerosis.
>
> But when "under a microscope" is added, the thickened intima no longer exists all by itself—but through the microscope. What is foregrounded through this addition is that the visibility of intimas depends on microscopes. And, for that matter, on a lot more. On the pointer. And on the two glass sheets that make the slide. Don't forget the decalcification that, even when it isn't done long enough, allows the technician to cut thin cross sections of a vessel. There's the work of that technician. The tweezers and the

knives. The dyes that turn the various cellular structures pink and purple. They are all required if pathologists are to see the thick intima of a vessel wall. (Mol, 2002, 30–31)

While in this excerpt the word "sociomateriality" is absent, the sociomateriality of medical practices is highly visible, both as a prerequisite and a result of medical action, and the same could be said for much of the STS-inspired literature on medicine and healthcare. Since the seminal special issue edited by Casper and Berg (1995) *Constructivist Perspectives on Medical Work: Medical Practices and Science and Technology Studies*, medical work has been framed in STS as "characterized by the ongoing articulation of highly heterogeneous elements and entities" (Casper & Berg, 1995, 399). In this scenario, the expression "sociomaterial/sociomateriality" was adopted quite naturally: in another seminal STS contribution on medicine, for example, Berg and Mol (1998, 6) described medical science as "a sociomaterial accomplishment, an in-situ achievement, a construction that necessarily remains local and rare."

What I am arguing is that the contribution of STS has been crucial in order to frame medicine and medical practice as a sociomaterial process in itself. Whereas in OS the concept of sociomateriality triggered an intense theoretical debate, in STS-oriented studies of medicine, it was a 'factual' idea, emerging from the observation of the everyday translations of medical abstract knowledge into medical practice. In these translations, scientific knowledge, protocols, and guidelines have to confront with material limitations of bodies, instruments, other conflicting protocols, and a variety of organizational settings (Schubert, 2011), so that the results may appear endlessly specific and surprising (Mol, 2002).

As for anything else in a sociomaterial approach, the very concept of sociomateriality may be enacted differently depending on the situation, and in fact, this is what we witness if we look at the ongoing debates and uses of the concept in OS and STS. To avoid essentialist conclusions and following a processual logic, my suggestion would then be to concentrate on what it 'does' the idea of sociomateriality more than on its definition.

2.5   A Sociomaterial Approach to Medical Work

I began this chapter by asking what is medical work 'made of.' I would like to conclude by focusing on what a sociomaterial approach 'does' to the study of what medical work is made of. In particular, I will suggest a sociomaterial approach points essentially to three arenas of which medical work is made of: (1) objects, technologies, and infrastructures; (2) language and communication; (3) organizational and professional knowledge, rules, and habits. Drawing on the idea that sociomateriality is a matter of degrees (Cooren, 2020), I will show how each of these arenas may be characterized by different degrees of materiality and sociality, but also how sociality and materiality always imply each other (although not always in a balanced proportion).

Objects, technologies, and infrastructures are the most prominent and immediately visible sociomaterial components of medical work, so that their degree of 'materiality' is usually higher than the 'social' one. But despite their materiality, objects, technologies, and infrastructures are mostly invisible to medical practitioners: they are "simply present" or just "transparent" forming the background to action and interaction (Bruni et al., 2007). Notoriously, this background emerges only at moments of breakdown, when its malfunctioning forcefully emphasizes its existence (Star, 1999). Passing from "matters of fact" to "matters of concern" (Latour, 2005), in these moments, the 'social' becomes more visible, as humans reorient their action in support of objects, technologies, and infrastructures (which cannot be taken for granted anymore). Typically, also the invisible work (Star & Strauss, 1999) actors perform to maintain and align the work of technologies with that of humans becomes more evident in these situations, as well as the relevance of actors' interpretations, speculations, and practical experience. Objects, technologies, and infrastructures always stand in relation to a situated organizational context, so that they give a clue for looking at the relations of which they are part, the practices in which they are located and which construct them socially, and the other materialities that cross their trajectories.

If objects, technologies, and infrastructures represent sociomaterial components of medical work with a high degree of materiality, the area of language and communication is probably the one with a highest score of sociality. Communication is the *medium* through which actors interact, asserting, discussing, and conflicting about what matters or counts in an organizational situation. Language and communication are constitutive of sensemaking processes in organizational activities (Weick, 1995), so that they are typically framed as pertaining to humans and intrinsically 'social.' By the way, as argued by the CCO approach (Cooren, 2004; Cooren et al., 2011), language and communication should not be reduced to symbolic or 'immaterial' acts taking place exclusively when people interact with each other. Talks, discourses, metaphors, texts, and narratives are performative (Latour, 1991), so that "one should examine what happens *in* and *through* communication to constitute, (re-)produce, or alter organizational forms and practices, whether these are policies, strategies, operations, values, (formal or informal) relations, or structures" (Cooren et al., 2011: 1151, italics in original). The materiality of language and communication can thus be seen in the concrete effects they produce. In this sense, communication becomes "the means by which organizations are established, composed, designed, and sustained" (Cooren et al., 2011: 1150). Moreover, language and communication are often 'material' in that they are grounded in texts, documents, signs, and so on (Bencherki, 2015), and they refer to various other materialities (objects, technologies, architectures). In this sense, the notion of textual agency (Cooren, 2004; Brummans, 2007) is crucial in order to recognize how "things make things with words" (Cooren & Bencherki, 2011). This means grasping how things may speak and enter the linguistic realm, pointing out not only how objects are being talked about in human conversations, but also how they concretely intervene in those conversations (Bencherki, 2015: 7).

The study of communication in medical practice has a longstanding tradition (Silverman, 1987; Cicourel, 1987), but in a sociomaterial approach, it is enriched by the idea that it is not an exclusive property of humans and that it has a shared nature (Nathues et al., 2020): medical guidelines and protocols 'speak' in the name of those who have elaborated and approved them; they are effective in that the actors who read and interpret them make them say how to act and whom should act; they make actors say that they are obliged to follow certain procedures, but this is also what actors make protocols and guidelines say. Thus, in language and communication, the social and the material are always entangled, and language is essential for the entanglement of the social and the material.

In medical settings, protocols and guidelines are also a good example of the sociomateriality of organizational and professional knowledge, rules, and habits. In terms of degrees, rules and habits are a good example of a mostly equal portion of the social and the material. Rules and habits are the product of human action and express institutionalized logics, values, and behaviors: from this point of view, they are eminently social. Over time, by the way, rules and habits become increasingly material, in that they are not perceived by organizational actors as outcomes of social processes, nor as fluid entities which can be easily changed: as for software (Leonardi, 2013), they transcend actors' control and become further 'objects' structuring organizational practices. Given the contingencies of medical work, by the way, a considerable portion of everyday work and interactions are oriented precisely to negotiating and articulating organizational and professional knowledge, rules, and habits. But given that in medical settings, rules and habits are constantly interpreted and adapted in relation to the situation or the problem at stake (Strauss et al., 1985; Casper & Berg, 1995), in so doing, they are turned into social objects again. But again, rules and habits may be heavier and stronger than situated interactions or interpretations, so that it may be that organizational actors use them as concrete and solid elements to which actors have to adapt. In this case, the material side of rules and habits further emerges.

The duality of rules and habits in professional and organizational settings has been widely acknowledged (March, 1988; March & Olsen, 1989), and in medical contexts, it typically recalls the use of protocols and guidelines, and/or the way knowledge is managed at the professional and the 'communitarian' level (Grosjean & Lacoste, 1999; Hindmarsh & Pilnick, 2002). To this cognitive stance, a sociomaterial perspective adds an explicit interest for the ways in which rules and habits are incorporated into bodies, technologies, and architectures, and in the relations that hold bodies and other materialities together. Studying the work of archaeologists, the context of a courtroom, an oceanographic research center, and a chemistry laboratory, Charles Goodwin (1994, 1995, 1996, 1997) has widely shown how tools, descriptions, definitions, words, and gestures work symbiotically. Standardized devices are useful and "functional" only when accompanied by human words and gestures. The relationship between objects and gestures is thus symbiotic, in that it gives rise to a whole that is different from the sum of its parts (the gesture + the object), and refers instead to the mutual interdependence of different elements (the "gesture-object," so to speak). In symbiotic gestures, Goodwin (2003, 20) argues, the objects of the gesture are integral components of the gesture itself. The professional vision (Goodwin, 1994) actors acquire and express in their everyday work is thus the outcome of the alignment of a series of socially and materially embodied practices, rather than the application of an abstract knowledge or automatic tool. Professional vision is essential to medical work (Goodwin, 2009, 2021; Gegenfurtner et al., 2019), in that practitioners learn to see the 'objects' with which they work (Goodwin, 1994: 606). From a sociomaterial point of view, in short, professional and organizational knowledge, rules and habits mirror the competence actors are supposed to have in aligning bodies and technologies.

The areas of technologies, communication, and organizational and professional knowledge will be 'operationalized' by means of various ethnographic data in the following of the book. Before that, the next chapter will present the methodology and the research design.

REFERENCES

Aanestad, M. (2003). The Camera as an Actor: Design-in-Use of Tele-medicine Infrastructure in Surgery. *Computer Supported Cooperative Work, 12*(1), 1–20.

Akrich, M. (1992). The De-scription of Technical Objects. In Bijker, W. & Law, & J. (eds.), *Shaping Technology/Building Society. Studies in Sociotechnical Change* (pp. 205–224). Cambridge, MA, MIT Press.

Barad, K. (2003). Posthumanist Performativity: Toward an Understanding of How Matter Comes to Matter. *Signs, 28*(3), 801–831.

Barad, K. (2007). *Meeting the Universe Halfway: Quantum Physics and the Entanglement of Matter and Meaning.* Duke University Press.

Becker, H., Geer, B., Hughes, E. C., & Strauss, A. (1961). *Boys in Whyte. Student culture in medical school.* University of Chicago Press.

Bencherki, N. (2015). *Spokesthings and phonation devices: How things make things do things with words.* Paper presented at the XXXI Egos Colloquium, Athens.

Berg, M. (1997). *Rationalizing Medical Work.* MIT Press.

Berg, M., & Mol, A. (Eds.). (1998). *Differences in Medicine: Unraveling Practices, Techniques and Bodies.* Duke University Press.

Berg, M., Horstman, K., Plass, S., & van Heusden, M. (2000). Guidelines, Professionals and the Production of Objectivity: Standardization and Professionalism of Insurance Medicine, *Sociology of Health & Illness,* 22(6), 765–91.

Brummans, B. (2007). Death by Document: Tracing the Agency of a Text. *Qualitative Inquiry, 13*(5), 711–727.

Bruni, A. (2005). Shadowing Software and Clinical Records: On the Ethnography of Non-humans and Heterogeneous Contexts. *Organization, 12*(3), 357–378.

Bruni, A. (2008). La medicina come ingegneria dell'eterogeneo e pratica socio-materiale. *Rassegna Italiana di Sociologia, XLIX*(3).

Bruni, A. (2015). Buster at Work: Intertwining Technology with Organizational and Working Practices. In A. Bruni, L. L. Parolin, & C. Schubert (Eds.), *Designing Technology, Work, Organization and Viceversa.* Vernon Press.

Bruni, A., Gherardi, S., & Parolin, L. (2007). Knowing in a System of Fragmented Knowledge. *Mind, Culture and Activity, 14*(1–2), 83–102.

Bruni, A., & Rizzi, C. (2013). Looking for Data in Diabetes Healthcare: Patient 2.0 and the Re-engineering of Clinical Encounters. *Science & Technology Studies, 26*(2), 29–43.

Callon, M. (1986). The Sociology of an Actor-Network: The Case of the Electric Vehicle. In M. Callon, J. Law, & A. Rip, Mapping the Dynamic of Science and Technology (pp. 19–34). : McMillan.

Callon, M. (1991). Techno-economic networks and irreversibility. In J. Law (Ed.), *A Sociology of Monsters: Essays on Power, Technology and Domination.* London, Routledge and Kegan Paul.

Carlile, P. R., Nicolini, D., Langley, A., & Tsoukas, H. (eds.) (2013). *How matter matters: Objects, artifacts, and materiality in organization studies*. Oxford, Oxford University Press.

Casper, M. (1994). Reframing and Grounding Nonhuman Agency: What Makes a Fetus an Agent? *American Behavioral Scientist, 37*, 839–856.

Casper, M. (1998). *The Making of the Unborn Patient: A Social Anatomy of Fetal Surgery*. Rutgers University Press.

Casper, M. J., & Berg, M. (1995). Constructivist Perspectives on Medical Work: Medical Practices and Science and Technology Studies. *Science, Technology, and Human Values, 20*, 395–407.

Cicourel, A. V. (1987). The Interpenetration of Communicative Contexts: Examples from Medical Encounters. *Social Psychology Quarterly, 50*, 217–226.

Cooren, F. (2004). Textual Agency: How Texts Do Things in Organizational Settings. *Organization, 11*(3), 373–393.

Cooren, F. (2020). Beyond Entanglement: (Socio-) Materiality and Organization Studies. *Organization Theory, 1*, 1–24.

Cooren, F., & Bencherki, N. (2011). How Things Do Things with Words: Ventriloquism, Passion and Technology. *Encyclopaideia, Journal of Phenomenology and Education, 28*, 35–61.

Cooren, F., Kuhn, T., Cornelissen, J. P., & Clark, T. (2011). Communication, Organizing and Organization: An Overview and Introduction to the Special Issue. *Organization Studies, 32*(9), 1149–1170.

Cussins, C. (1998). Ontological Choreography: Agency for Women Patients in an Infertility Clinic. In M. Berg & A.-M. Mol (Eds.), *Differences in Medicine* (pp. 166–201). Duke University Press.

Elston, M. A. (1997). *The Sociology of Medical Science and Technology*. Blackwell.

Epstein, S. S. (1978). *The Politics of Cancer*, San Francisco: Sierra Club Books.

Foucault, M. (1963). *Naissance de la clinique: une archéologie du regard médical*, Paris: Presses universitaires de France(engl. trans., *The Birth of the Clinic: An Archaeology of Medical Perception, Pantheon Books*, 1973). London: Routledge

Freidson, E. (1970). *Professional Dominance: The Social Structure of Medical Care*. Aldine.

Gegenfurtner, A., Lehtinen, E., Helle, L., Nivala, M., Svedström, E., & Säljö, R. (2019). Learning to See Like an Expert: On the Practices of Professional Vision and Visual Expertise. *International Journal of Educational Research, 98*, 280–291.

Gibson, J. G. (1979). *The Ecological Approach to Visual Perception*. Houghton-Mifflin.

Glaser, B., & Strauss, A. (1965). *Awareness of Dying*. Aldine.

Goffman, E. (1961). *Asylums: Essays on the Social Situation of Mental Patients and Other Inmates*. Doubleday.

Goodwin, C. (1994). Professional Vision. *American Anthropologist, 3*, 606–633.

Goodwin, C. (1995). Seeing in Depth, in *Social Studies of Science*, 25, pp. 237–274.

Goodwin, C. (1996). Practices of Color Classification. *Ninchi Kagaku, 2*, 62–82.

Goodwin, C. (1997). The Blackness of Black. In L. Resnik, C. Saljo, C. Pontecorvo, & B. Burge (Eds.), *Discourse, Tools and Reasoning. Essays on Situated Cognition* (pp. 111–140). Springer Verlag.

Goodwin, C. (2003). The Body in Action. In J. Coupland & R. Gwyn (Eds.), *Discourse, the Body and Identity* (pp. 19–42). Palgrave Macmillan.

Goodwin, D. (2009). *Acting in Anaesthesia. Ethnographic Encounters with Patients, Practitioners and Medical Technologies.* Cambridge University Press.

Goodwin, D. (2021). Describing Failures of Healthcare: A Study in the Sociology of Knowledge. *Qualitative Research, 21*(3), 324–340.

Grosjean, M., & Lacoste, M. (1999). *Communication et Intelligence collective. Le Travail à l'Hopital.* PUF.

Haraway, D. J. (1988). Situated Knowledges: The Science Question in Feminism and the Privilege of Partial Perspective. *Feminist Studies, 14*(3), 575–599.

Haraway, D. (1991). *Simians, Cyborgs, and Women: The Reinvention of Nature.* Routledge.

Harré, R. (2002). Material Objects in Social Worlds. *Theory, Culture and Society, 19*, 23–36.

Hindmarsh, J., & Pilnick, A. (2002). The Tacit Order of Teamwork: Collaboration and Embodied Conduct in Anesthesia. *The Sociological Quarterly, 43*, 139–164.

Hui, S., Shove, E., & Schatzki, T. (Eds.). (2016). *The Nexus of Practices: Connections, Constellations, and Practitioners.* Routledge.

Illich, I. (1976). *Medical Nemesis: The Expropriation of Health.* London, Marion Boyars.

Jones, M. (2014). A Matter of Life and Death: Exploring Conceptualizations of Sociomateriality in the Context of Critical Care. *MIS Quarterly, 38*(3), 895–925.

Knorr Cetina, K. (1997). Sociality with Objects, *Theory, Culture and Society, 14*, 1–30.

Latour, B. (1988). *The Pasteurization of France.* Harvard University Press.

Latour, B. (1990). Drawing Things Together. In M. Lynch, S. Woolgar (Eds.), *Representation in Scientific Practice* (pp. 19–68). Cambridge, MIT Press.

Latour, B. (1991). The Impact of Science Studies on Political Philosophy. *Science, Technology, & Human Values, 16*, 3–19.

Latour, B. (1992), Where are the missing masses, sociology of a few mundane artefacts. In W. Bijker and J. Law (eds), *Shaping Technology-Building Society. Studies in Sociotechnical Change* (pp. 225–259). MIT Press, Cambridge MA.

Latour, B. (2002). Morality and Technology. The End of the Means, *Theory, Culture and Society, 19*, 247–60.

Latour, B. (2005). *Reassembling the Social. An Introduction to Actor-Network Theory.* Oxford University Press.

Law, J. (1987). Technologies and Heterogeneous Engineering: The Case of the Portuguese Expansion. In W.E. Bijker, T.P. Hughes, T.J. Pinch, The Social Construction of Technical Systems: New Directions in the Sociology and History of Technology (pp. 111–133). MIT Press.

Law, J. (1992). Notes on the Theory of the Actor-Network: Ordering, Strategy and Heterogeneity. *System/Practice, 5*, 379–93.

Law, J. (1994). *Organizing Modernity*. Blackwell.

Law, J. (2001). Machinic Pleasures and Interpellations. Centre for Science Studies, Lancaster University, Lancaster LA1 4YN, UK, accessed 8/25/2016 at http://www.comp.lancs.ac.uk/sociology/papers/Law-Machinic-Pleasures-and-Interpellations.pdf

Law, J. (2007). Making a mess with method. In W. Outhwaite, S. P. Turner (eds.), *The Sage Handbook of Social Science Methodology* (pp. 595–606). London, Sage.

Law, J. (2009). Actor Network Theory and Material Semiotics. In B.S. Turner (ed.), *The New Blackwell Companion to Social Theory* (pp. 141–158). Chichester, Wiley-Blackwell.

Law, J. (2019). *Material Semiotics*. Retrieved from www.heterogeneities.net/publications/Law2019MaterialSemiotics.pdf

Law, J., & Mol, A. (1995). Notes on Materiality and Sociality. *Sociological Review, 43*(2), 274–294.

Leonardi, P. M. (2012). Materiality, Sociomateriality, and Socio-Technical Systems: What Do These Terms Mean? How Are They Related? Do We Need Them. In P. M. Leonardi, B. A. Nardi, & J. Kallinikos (Eds.), *Materiality and Organizing: Social Interaction in a Technological World* (pp. 25–48). Oxford University Press.

Leonardi, P. M. (2013). Theoretical Foundations for the Study of Sociomateriality. *Information and Organization, 23*(2), 59–76.

March, J. G. (1988). *Decisions and Organizations*. Basil Blackwell.

March, J., & Olsen, J. P. (1989). *Rediscovering Institutions. The Organizational Basis of Politics*. Free Press.

Mol, A. (2002). *The Body Multiple: Ontology in Medical Practice*. Duke University Press.

Mol, A., Moser, I., & Pols, J. (2010). Care: putting practice into theory. In A.Mol, I. Moser, J. Pols, (eds.), *Care in Practice. On Tinkering in Clinics, Homes and Farms* (pp. 7–27). Transcript, Verlag, Bielefeld.

Moreira, T. (2005). Diversity in Clinical Guidelines: The Role of Repertoires of Evaluation, *Social Science and Medicine, 62*(4), 1022–30.

Nathues, E., van Vuuren, M., & Cooren, F. (2020). Speaking About Vision, Talking in the Name of so Much More: A Methodological Framework for Ventriloquial Analyses in Organization Studies. *Organization Studies, 42*, 1457–1476.

Orlikowski, W. J. (2007). Sociomaterial Practices: Exploring Technology at Work. *Organization Studies, 28*(9), 1435–1448.

Orlikowski, W. J., & Scott, S. V. (2008). Sociomateriality: Challenging the Separation of Technology. *Work and Organization, The Academy of Management Annals*, 2(1), 433–474.

Parsons, T. (1951). Illness and the Role of the Phisician: A Sociological Perspective. *American Journal of Psychiatry*, 21, 452–60.

Pickering, A. (1995). *The Mangle of Practice: Time, Agency, and Science*. Chicago, University of Chicago Press.

Schubert, C. (2011). Making Sure. A Comparative Micro-analysis of Diagnostic Instruments in Medical Practice. *Social Science & Medicine*, 73(6), 851–857.

Silverman, D. (1987). *Communication in Medical Practice*. Sage.

Star, S. L. (1991). Invisible Work and Silenced Dialogues in Knowledge Representation. In I. Eriksson, B. Kitchenham, & K. Tijdens, Women, Work and Computerization (pp. 81–92). : North Holland.

Star, S. L. (1996). Working Together: Symbolic Interactionism, Activity Theory and Information Systems. In Y. Engestrom, D. Middleton (eds.), *Cognition and Communication at Work*, Cambridge, Cambridge University Press.

Star, S. L. (1999). The Ethnography of the Infrastructure. *American Behavioral Scientist*, 43, 377–391.

Star, S. L., & Strauss, A. (1999). Layers of Silence, Arenas of Voice: The Ecology of Visible and Invisible Work. *Computer-Supported Cooperative Work*, 8(1/2), 9–30.

Strauss, A., Fagerhaugh, S., Suczek, B., & Wiener, C. (1985). *The Social Organization of Medical Work*. University of Chicago Press.

Suchman, L. (2000). Organizing Alignment: A Case of Bridge-Building. *Organization*, 7(2), 311–327.

Suchman, L. (2002). Located accountabilities in technology production. *Scandinavian Journal of Management*, 14(2), 91–105.

Suchman, L. (2007). *Human–machine Reconfigurations: Plans and Situated Actions*. Cambridge University Press.

Sudnow, D. (1967). *Passing On: The Social Organization of Dying*. Prentice-Hall.

Thompson, C. (2005). *Making Parents: The Ontological Choreography of Reproductive Technologies*. MIT Press.

Timmermans, S., & Berg, M. (2003). The Practice of Medical Technology. *Sociology of Health and Illness*.

Timmermans, S., & Berg, M. (2004). *The Gold Standard: The Challenge of Evidence-based Medicine and Standardization in Health Care*. Temple University Press.

Turner, B. S. (1987). *Medical Power and Social Knowledge*. London and New Delhi, Sage.

Turner, B. S. (1992). *Regulating Bodies. Essays in Medical Sociology*. London and New York: Routledge.

Weick, K. E. (1995). *Sensemaking in Organizations*. Sage.

CHAPTER 3

The Research Setting: Doing Ethnography in the Operating Room

Abstract This chapter presents the methodology and the empirical research context. The chapter illustrates organizational ethnography in theory and in practice, focusing in particular on the challenges triggered by a sociomaterial approach. The empirical context is represented by the operating block of a hospital located in a medium-sized province of the north of Italy. In order to observe everyday work, different actors of the operating block were shadowed on a weekly basis, for a total of eight weeks. Independently of the operator observed, the shadowing activity located the observations within the same organizational space (the operating unit with its various rooms). This yielded ethnographic accounts that conveyed both the various work practices and professional visions to which actors might refer.

Keywords Organizational ethnography • Shadowing • Interview to the double • Sociomateriality

3.1 THE RESEARCH SETTING

The data I will present were part of a broader research project conducted by the Dept. of Sociology and Social Research of the University of Trento together with the local Agency for Healthcare Services (Agenzia Provinciale per i Servizi Sanitari—APSS) focused on the construction of organizational safety in operating room (Bruni, 2010).

Given the explicit willingness of the organization in using the research as an opportunity to reconsider some of the work processes and aiming at gradually approaching the activity of the operating room, at the very beginning, we approached the already existing "Operating Room Process Analysis Document" in use in the department where the observations would have taken place. This document contains a detailed description of the activities, the professional roles, and the related competences. Its review allowed on the one hand to have an initial knowledge of the formal structuring of work and organizational processes, and on the other to update and refine the knowledge codified at the organizational level.

Five semi-structured interviews were then conducted with highly experienced actors, so to start reconstructing the daily work in the operating room from the point of view of the actors involved. The interview concluded by asking the interviewee to imagine s/he had to instruct her/his 'double' in to perform her§/his daily work without anyone noticing the exchange. This is what is known as the 'interview to the double' (Gherardi, 1990; Bruni & Gherardi, 2001), a particular type of interview technique aimed at stimulating actors to reflect on their everyday work practices, but also on the relational activities implied by work practices, thus offering a reading of work and organizing as a joint result of the two. The data generated by this interview technique allow researchers to look into the details of interviewees' everyday activities, eliciting the situated knowledge connected to such activities (Nicolini, 2009).

This initial phase made possible to familiarizing with the salient steps of the operating process and the technical language in use among operators, so to enter the operating room aware of the main procedures and of the technical and professional jargon in use.

3.2   Organizational Ethnography

Organizational ethnography aims at describing and interpreting the everyday processes of organizing, adopting a research methodology based on *in situ* observation of organizational life, and taking a symbolic-interpretive perspective (Hatch, 2019) to the study of organizations. From this perspective, organizations are social artifacts, collective inventions kept alive through actions, languages, symbols, rituals, technologies, objects, and expert knowledge. In short, through a series of elements that, especially in their whole, "make" organization. Organizations are framed as "processual phenomena emerging from the intentional acts of people acting individually or together with others" (Strati, 1996: 72), that is, as arenas of a negotiated (dis)order (Weick, 1976). Everyday organizational interactions and practices represent the privileged unit of analysis in order to provide a thick description (Geertz, 1973) of organizational life; that is, a "dense" illustration of the observed environment and processes.

While early organizational ethnographies focused mainly on the cultural and symbolic aspects of organizational life, over the years, an ethnographic approach has been used in relation to a variety of aspects, taking on different accents and nuances depending on the perspective in which the organizational phenomenon has been interpreted. Over the years, organizational ethnographies have thus helped to highlight the plurality and contradictory nature of organizational cultures (Martin, 1992); the dynamic role of shared symbols, artifacts, and rituals (Manning, 1992); the tacit, aesthetic, and common-sense knowledge that informs organizational action (Strati, 1992, 1999); the role performed by technologies in organizational action (Engeström & Middleton, 1996); as well as the construction of gender and diversity as a practical and situated activity (Bruni et al., 2005).

Because of its situatedness and context dependency, ethnography implies a flexible research design (Silverman, 1997). Nevertheless, organizational ethnography typically focuses on:

- the physical structure of the organization: the outward appearance of the organization, the location of spaces and departments, the presence or absence of common spaces, the furniture, and the technologies present are all elements that have functional and symbolic significance and contribute to forming a system of meanings that defines the identity and activity of the various organizational actors;
- the social structure of the organization: the relationships between actors, roles, hierarchies, departments, and divisions, and thus the way in which the organization internally manages the division of labor. This includes the organizational chart, the number of people in the organization, the tasks of those people (as planned by the organization), as well as the various relationships (functional and otherwise) that bind actors together;

- the interactions among organizational actors: these concern the ways in which people relate to each other on the basis of their organizational roles and in day-to-day interactions. The interest, however, is not in what distinguishes formal from informal interactions, but in how actors attribute meaning to their own and others' actions, whether formal or informal;
- the language of organizational actors: the jargon and linguistic expressions in use within everyday interactions.

Traditionally, the research techniques that organizational ethnography employs (above all, participant observation and in-depth interviewing) imply a prolonged presence of the researcher in the field. In contemporary debate, however, organizational ethnography has become an umbrella concept under which can be found studies conducted with different data collection techniques and time management. There are cases in which the fieldwork may not be particularly intensive but protracted for entire years (Kunda, 1992; Barley & Kunda, 2004); others in which several months are spent in the field, but in immersive terms (Bruni & Gherardi, 2001; Bruni et al., 2005); and still others in which the timing of fieldwork is indeed limited, but focused toward the observation of specific activities and complemented by a good background knowledge of the research field (Knoblauch, 2005).

While there is no agreement on how much time should a researcher spend in the field in order to claim to have conducted an ethnography, from a practical point of view, the dilemma disappears. The question does not regard how long an ethnography should last in theory, but the ability of the researcher in coming to an in-depth understanding of the field observed.

3.3   Doing Ethnography, Looking for Sociomateriality

Ethnographic techniques are essential to grasp the sociomateriality of organizational practices. In this regard, Mol (2002) has proposed the expression "praxiography" ("a story about practices") when studying the doings of atherosclerosis, or rather the many ways in which atherosclerosis is brought into being through technologies, diagnostic devices, protocols, work, and organizational practices. In her words: "an ethnographer/

praxiographer out to investigate diseases never isolates these from the practices in which they are, what one may call, *enacted*. She stubbornly takes notice of the techniques that make things visible, audible, tangible, knowable. She may talk bodies—but she never forgets about microscopes" (Mol, 2002: 33, emphasis in original).

Marko Niemimaa (2014) has explicitly focused on why and how ethnography fits a sociomaterial approach. In his view, "in order to accurately conceptualize the sociomateriality of a phenomenon, it is imperative to immerse into the context. The researcher needs to understand the material discursive nature of the context [...]. Long-term studies using observations are thus appropriate approaches" (Niemimaa, 2014, p. 7). By the way, a sociomaterial stance toward ethnography requires to challenge and to expand the conceptual toolbox of what the author defines as "interpretive ethnography," referring to the ethnographic tradition we inherited from anthropology (Geertz, 1973) and sociology (Atkinson, 1990; Silverman, 1997). In particular, a sociomaterial ethnography differs from an interpretive one in that (Niemimaa, 2014):

1. sociomaterial ethnography starts from the premise that the world is not socially constructed, but that it is the result of various (and more or less durable) sociomaterial entanglements. The phenomenon at stake, thus, is not the social construction of reality, but the sociomaterial entanglements that make reality 'real.' This reflects to the attention sociomaterial ethnographers pay not only to how objects and technologies acquire meanings, but also to how these meanings materialize and to how they are materially sustained (Schultze, 2011). As from Barad (2007), meanings and interpretations are always material-discursive, in that they refer to the material conditions that make a speech act or a concept intelligible;

2. assuming reality is in becoming and that it materializes in a multitude of forms that are not simply given in nature, sociomaterial ethnography shifts the researcher sensitivity from representation to performativity. That is, from a vision of the world (and of the field of observation) as stable and ready to be investigated, to a messier configuration (Law, 2004) in which "reality is defined as things-in-phenomena and not as things-in-themselves" (Gherardi, 2017: 44). Since the linguistic turn (Marcus & Cushman, 1982; Clifford, 1983), the performativity of language and of ethnographic accounts has long been debated, but how to account for the flow of activities

that transform 'something' into 'a thing' is a different issue. Writing performative accounts requires a vocabulary that prefers verbs to nouns, and which traces the continued connections that take place between a variety of material and semiotic elements. As from Latour (2005), a good account is an account which traces networks and an agent is such only if and when she/he/it performs an action;

3. whereas in traditional ethnography the researcher was seen as a professional stranger (Agar, 1980) and in postmodern ethnography as a bricoleur (Manning, 1995), in sociomaterial ethnography, researchers are part of the phenomenon studied, in that it is precisely through their agential cuts and intra-actions that phenomena emerge. In this regard, Latour (2005) has proposed the adoption of an "infra-language," a language able to situate the researcher and the reader within the practices described and which combine to form the phenomenon being investigated. For sociomaterial ethnographers, thus, this means considering not only the essential reflexivity of ethnographic descriptions and interpretations (Garfinkel, 1967), but also their accountability and responsibility. Given that in a sociomaterial perspective agency is not a property of humans or nonhumans but "the enactment of iterative changes to particular practices through the dynamics of intra-activity" (Barad, 2003, p. 827), researchers should be able to account and to take the responsibility for their practices, as they cannot be separated from the phenomenon at stake. In other words, "ethnographic researcher has to be sensitive to the cuts she/he helps to enact" (Niemimaa, 2014, p. 8).

The following table (Table 3.1) summarizes the main differences between an interpretive and a sociomaterial ethnography.

Given these methodological premises, we will now focus on shadowing, the main observational technique adopted for gathering data.

3.4   Shadowing: Following Practices

The core of the research entailed the direct observation of organizational and work practices in the operating room. Observations have been conducted through the shadowing technique, whose main characteristic resides in 'accompanying' (like a shadow, so to say) a subject in the course of his/her everyday organizational and work activity. At large, shadowing refers to an observational technique used to gather data about

Table 3.1 Main differences between interpretive and sociomaterial ethnography (adapted from Niemimaa, 2014, p. 6)

	Interpretive ethnography	*Sociomaterial ethnography*
Ontological assumption	Reality is socially constructed	Reality is the effect of sociomaterial entanglements
Phenomenon of interest	Social interaction	Sociomaterial entanglements
Type of knowledge	Representative	Performative
Role of researcher	In distant/close relation to the phenomenon	Part of the phenomenon
Positioning of the researcher	Reflexive	Accountable and responsible

'on-the-ground' phenomena within predetermined periods of time (Sachs, 1993). At whatever level of observation, it yields a combination of documentary data on how people engage in their everyday activities, individual and collective (Bruni et al., 2005).

The trajectory of this research technique is somehow peculiar: while practiced since ever in ethnographic studies (also *Street Corner Society* could be taken as an example of shadowing—Becker, 2002, personal communication),[1] it has only recently become an explicit object of attention and reflection for sociologists and organizational researchers. The turning point of this trajectory is probably represented by the publication in 2007 of Barbara Czarniawska's book *Shadowing and Other Techniques for Doing Fieldwork in Modern Societies*. Here, she nicely reconstructs the origins and the characteristics of shadowing, systematizing the scattered existing literature and referring to hers and other researchers' experiences in order to offer a practical understanding of it. Moreover, she connects shadowing to a number of other issues at the center of the organizational and ethnographic debate: the 'practice turn' (Schatzki et al., 2001); the 'turn to objects' (Engeström & Blackler, 2005); the definition of 'the field' in an increasingly scattered and networked society; and the

---

[1] In 2002, I had the chance to meet Howard Becker in Trento in the occasion of the opening of a new PhD program. At that time, I was involved in various ethnographic projects (Bruni & Gherardi, 2001; Bruni et al., 2005; Bruni, 2005), all based on shadowing. Having difficulties in finding literature on it, I took the occasion to ask Howard Becker for some references, but to his knowledge there were not that many, in that was a kind of "taken for granted technique" (as he defined it)

contribution STS (mainly in their ANT version) can offer thanks to their insisting on a symmetric treatment of all "actants" (Callon, 1986) involved in an action net (Czarniawska, 2004). In so doing, Czarniawska shows the 'urgency' of the adoption of shadowing for the social sciences, elevating it (a few years later) to "the best field technique in management and organization studies" (Czarniawska, 2014).

It is no coincidence, thus, if after 2007 shadowing becomes institutionalized in the social and organizational research as a new observational technique in its own right. Mintzberg's structured observation of the working week of five managers (Mintzberg, 1973) is usually quoted in organization studies as a kind of shadowing *ante litteram*, whereas in sociology, the shadowing technique has often been referred to a novel by Truman Capote (*A Day's Work*, 1975) in which he narrates his experience of following for an entire working day a cleaning woman (Sclavi, 1989). Thus, as it is common in the history of innovations, the origins of shadowing are dispersed across a variety of places and 'inventors' not necessarily aware of each other's work (Czarniawska, 2007). And, as it is common in a process of institutionalization, the more an activity is considered as 'legitimate,' the more a set of rules and a common practice is needed. We can thus refer to the ten practical rules suggested by Gill et al. (2014):

1. *Proactively engage with shadowees ahead of time.* Shadowing entails a constant and intrusive relationship between the researcher and the subject shadowed, so that it is crucial to discuss beforehand how to balance the needs of the shadowee and the interest of the researcher;
2. *Reflect on the emotional side of qualitative methods.* As for any kind of immersive ethnography, one may be prepared to handle the methodological aspects of conducting research but not the emotional labor or the ethical dilemmas it entails;
3. *Prepare for embodied shadowing.* Shadowing is a physically and mentally demanding activity, as it can easily take to entire days of observation per entire working weeks. "Preparing for shadowing means recognizing that it is material" (Gill et al., 2014: 16), as it engages researchers fully with their bodies;
4. *Pack a "shadow kit."* A notebook, one or more pens, a smartphone, a voice recorder, a bottle of water, some cash, one's own identity card, and, sometimes, a uniform, a badge, or dedicated clothes: shadowing is material also because it articulates through a plethora of objects, which constitute the material infrastructure of the researcher activity;

5. *Plan to follow the rules, at first.* Even the more experienced shadower is always a novice when entering a new field. In order to be accepted, s/he has to quickly learn the main rules and taken for granted of the social world s/he is in and respect them in order not to be perceived as an element of disturbance and/or an incompetent participant;

6. *Play around with strategies for notetaking.* Taking notes is essential, but it requires to take decisions about what kind of notes to take, when, and where. As ethnographers well know, taking notes is a highly subjective activity which can be managed in a variety of ways, highly depending on the concrete situations the researcher finds her/himself in (Vasquez et al., 2012). Thus, it is necessary to find a balance between the need of taking notes and the importance of continuously pay attention to what continues to happen while writing down notes.

7. *Dance in the doldrums.* In sailing, the term "doldrums" refers to no wind times, so that sailors can rest. Shadowing can offer moments of "doldrums" which can be fruitfully implied by the researcher for mentally and physically relax a bit, review previous notes, write up episodes s/he did not detail, prepare questions to address in the future, re-read notes, and start advancing interpretations;

8. *Locate or create social support.* Shadowing is a solitary activity, but precisely because of that the researcher has to find ways to 'share' the tensions and the ethical doubts emerging from the fieldwork. Having the possibility to confront with somebody (a colleague or a friend) or simply having somebody willing to listening may be of great help for slow down tensions deriving from observations;

9. *Mitigate the anticipation of shadower-as-betrayer.* Shadowing takes the researcher close to participants' lives in such an intimate way that at the end of the research shadowees may feel betrayed by the descriptions of the researcher. As the head of a hospital department once said to me, reading the final research report he had the feeling of looking at a naked portrait of himself. Thus, it can be a good idea to anticipate to participants the kind of episodes, thoughts, and interpretations the researcher is going to show, also as a way to be sure not to harm them;

10. *Exit the field mindfully.* As for every ethnography, leaving the field is a delicate moment (Hammersley & Atkinson, 1995). It is important for the researcher to submit the final account of the research to the shadowed people, to gather their opinions, not to "run away"

from the field but to handle the moment of exit as carefully as s/he did in negotiating access, and to demonstrate a willingness to confront the organization about the interpretations provided.

Besides these common practical indications, I would stress that from my perspective, the distinguishing characteristic of shadowing resides in its situatedness. When following another person as his/her shadow, the meanings and interpretations that the researcher may give to that person's actions are 'emerging' from the shadowing activity itself, and they do not necessarily have to be related to a broader cultural context. Shadowing constitutes 'in and of itself' a situation in which the persons concerned have to negotiate their mutual engagement on the basis of different practices, thereby enabling each of them (including the researcher) to 'perform' their everyday understandings and routines (Bruni et al., 2005). Although qualitative sociology has often emphasized the distance that separates (or should separate) the situation observed and the observer (Burgess, 1988), as well as a certain 'neutrality' in the latter's behavior (Agar, 1980). On the contrary, shadowers usually conduct their fieldwork preferring to behave as 'intruders' rather than as 'outsiders.' This means interpreting the shadowing not in the static sense of a reflecting surface, but rather in processual terms, as an opaque body interposed between the light and the object illuminated; as an indistinct or vaguely defined figure who generated misunderstanding, curiosity, or suspicion. Shadows, for that matter, tend to distort the shapes that they reflect, according to the light and to the backdrop on which they are projected (Bruni et al., 2005).

In accordance with a sociomaterial understanding of ethnography, at the writing stage, this kind of fieldwork behavior gives rise to ethnographic accounts which not only situate the researcher within the action contexts observed, but constitute units of action/interaction on which to focus during analysis and theoretical sensemaking. In fact, concurring with the idea that any social situation can be studied as self-organizing with respect to its manifestations (Heritage, 1984), actors (researcher and participating subjects) and events may be seen as 'accomplishments' (Schütz, 1932): dynamic and reconstructible social facts which constitute the practices and discourses subject to investigation.

In this sense, it should be bear in mind that the objective of shadowing is not the reconstruction of the individual profile of a particular organizational actor, but rather the observation of everyday organizational life, starting from the sharing of a certain perspective and array of practices (those performed by the person one is shadowing). As much as 'shadows' of individual actors, indeed, the researchers nevertheless maintain an attitude of diffuse attention (Bruni et al., 2005) on the organizational processes and work practices in which the actor they were following was involved, rather than on the latter's personality.

Starting from the reconstruction of the daily work practices of each practitioner, it was thus possible to grasp and understand the way in which a heterogeneity of processes and practices takes shape.

3.5   THE RESEARCH DESIGN: SHADOWING ORGANIZATIONAL AND WORK PRACTICES IN THE OPERATING ROOM

As anticipated, the empirical context of the research is represented by the operating unit of a hospital located in a medium-to-small-sized province of the north-east of Italy. In order to observe everyday work, different actors of the operating block were shadowed on a weekly basis, for a total of eight weeks. In particular, the first five weeks were spent shadowing the actors involved in a surgical équipe, namely:

- 1 room staff nurse;
- 1 nurse anesthetist;
- 1 instrument nurse;
- 1 anesthesiologist;
- 1 surgeon.

The last three weeks were dedicated to the shadowing of:

- 1 entering instrument nurse;
- the Head instrument nurse;
- the Head of the operating block nurses.

The decision of shadowing the two Head nurses was made in order to open a window on the work that took place outside the physical space of the operating theatre, on the assumption that the processes and practices in the operating room were interconnected with processes and practices occurring in other spaces and times (Czarniawska, 2004).

The shadowing for a week of a 'novice' was instead dictated by the desire to observe the practices whereby the work and routine organizational processes were transmitted and learned (Lave & Wenger, 1991). In general, flanking novices typically allows ethnographers to engage with a range of issues and uncertainties experienced by those who, not entirely familiar with an activity, do not take it for granted and therefore require constant instructions on what to do. The shadowing of novices thus mitigates the sense of being a 'fish out of cultural water' (Schwartz & Jacobs, 1979) or a 'secret apprentice' (Garfinkel, 1967) often felt by ethnographers. It is the novices themselves who ask the (banal) questions that the researchers would like to ask (and/or who need continuous explicit instructions on everyday work practices). This makes it possible to collect detailed accounts without having to interrupt the flow of everyday work (and/or take excessive advantage of the patience of the actors being observed).

Independently of the operator observed, the shadowing activity located the observations within the same organizational space (the operating unit with its various rooms). This yielded ethnographic accounts that conveyed both the various work practices to which actors might refer, and the specificity of the climate and the interactions that developed in the setting observed.

The shadowing was carried out by myself and a PhD student (Giusi Orabona) I was starting tutoring at that time.[2] Shadowing-in-two implied a tight coordination between the two researchers: fieldnotes were shared and discussed between the two researchers, who met weekly to update (and listen to) each other about the main events and impressions.

As in any ethnographic research, the stay in the field offered the opportunity to have numerous and repeated informal conversations with different organizational actors, which thus also generated expectations in the participants with respect to the results of the research. Starting with a preliminary analysis of the data collected, it was then decided to conduct a number of meetings with some of the actors involved by the shadowing. During these meetings, different lived episodes recorded during the fieldwork and representative of organizational dynamics and working practices in the operating room were proposed to the participants. These meetings thus allowed for further exploring the range of meanings that different practitioners attribute to their daily work, as well as to 'test' some of the

---

[2] I thank Giusi Orabona for the work conducted with me and for sharing with me her observations. In the case of this book, however, I mainly refer to my own observations and only in a few cases to those written by Giusi.

interpretations regarding the processes observed and to verify the meaningfulness of these interpretations for the organizational actors involved.

3.6 ENTERING AN ORGANIZATIONAL ETHNOGRAPHY, MEETING EVERYDAY WORK

In the pages to follow, readers will be introduced inside the Operating Block of a hospital in northern Italy. Description and interpretation will continue in parallel, and readers will encounter a text constructed both through analytical reasoning and through the channels of evocation and empathetic relationship with the reality described. In this way, a different relationship is established between text and readers, in which the logic of the narrative replaces the objectivity of the scientific gaze, without the claim of exhaustiveness (Bruni et al., 2005). In short, an attempt has been made to write a text capable of engaging readers in a learning relationship, within which it is the readers themselves who have the opportunity to interpret the meaning of events through the flow of the narrative. The personal names that will be encountered are fictional in order to clothe the subjects involved with anonymity. Where the narrative allowed, moreover, I have chosen to refer only to the organizational role played by the people involved in the interaction ('doctor,' 'operator,' 'user,' 'patient,' 'nurse,' and so on).

Given these premises, and before we finally dive into the ethnographic notes, we can start by looking at what usually happens in the course of a surgery session in the operating room.

From an organizational point of view, the start of a surgery can be identified in the moment when the nurse anesthetist tells the room staff nurse that the operating room is ready and that the patient can be transferred from the ward to the room. The room staff nurse thus reaches the phone in front of the sterilization room, calls the ward, and asks to transport the patient to the room.

Meanwhile, the instrument nurse also enters the room and (after saying goodbye) reads the operating list and asks the room staff nurse to take the container with the irons needed for the first surgery. It may also happen, however, that the operating list is not in the room because the room staff nurse has brought it with her/him (to read the patients' names). In that case, the nurse anesthetist will wait for the list to know the exact number of scheduled surgeries and the type of anesthesia planned. While waiting, she will prepare a few drips (usually, four).

Once the operating list is read, the instrument and nurse anesthetist discuss the positioning of the patient. In most of the cases, the decision is made by mutual agreement, but it may also be the case that the instrument nurse has a different opinion from the nurse anesthetist and, therefore, they wait until the surgeons arrive and leave the decision to them. This discussion can take place either before the patient arrives or after, depending on the type of surgery (if particularly complex, it is more common to wait for the surgeons' opinion).

The instrument nurse at this point goes to wash up and then returns to the room. Here, the room staff nurse is waiting for her to "dress" her and to help her placing the instruments on the sterile iron table. Both workers are now wearing protective masks. The anesthesiologist and surgeons, however, are not present.

When the patient reaches the preoperative area (on a stretcher, carried by the room staff nurse), the nurse anesthetist approaches him/her, smiles, and introduces her/himself. Calling the patient by name (after looking at the operating list), the nurse anesthetist explains to the patient that s/he is about to insert a drip into his arm. After the drip is inserted, the nurse anesthetist asks the patient how much pain s/he felt on a scale from 0 to 10 (where 0 means "no pain" and 10 means "unbearable pain"). To the patient's answer (which almost always corresponds to a number ranging from 0 to 3), the nurse anesthetist replies by saying that s/he will ask this same question at the end of the procedure so that s/he can decide whether or not to administer pain relief. The patient nods and the nurse anesthetist (again in the preoperative area) finishes preparing the drips for the next scheduled patients.

The anesthesiologist enters the operating room and, after looking at the operating list, heads to the preoperative area, greets the patient, and introduces her/himself. After explanations regarding preparation for surgery, the anesthesiologist asks the patient a series of questions related to her/his medical history ("Have you had surgery before? Do you have any allergies? Is this your first anesthesia? How much does he weigh? Does he take blood pressure pills? Is he a smoker? Has he ever had any lung problems?") and has her/him sign the anesthesia consent.

Once the preparation is completed (in the preoperative area), if the patient is able to walk, s/he is accompanied by the nurse anesthetist to the operating room; otherwise, s/he is transported on a stretcher by room staff nurse and the nurse anesthetist. Once s/he reaches the operating room, the room staff nurse and the nurse anesthetist help her/him to position her/himself on the bed, or to move from the stretcher to the operating bed. The nurse anesthetist straps her/his arm to the armrest of the bed, measures her/his pressure, and asks her/him if the position is comfortable (to this question, the patient always answers affirmatively).

Usually, the surgeons are not in the room yet when the nurse anesthetist sits on a stool placed near the ventilator and fills out the anesthesiology chart, while the anesthesiologist leaves the room. It may happen, however, that surgeons are already in the preoperative area even before the instrument nurse has finished preparing the sterile irons, or before the patient is placed on the operating table (when the surgery is particularly complex, or when it is the last one of the day). In either cases, the surgeons will urge the operators to complete the room preparation as quickly as possible; urging to which the operators will easily respond in an annoyed tone.

If the surgeons have already washed up (or if they are in the process of doing so), the anesthesiologist enters the room and begins the induction of anesthesia; if the surgeons have not arrived yet, the anesthesiologist will chat a bit with the nurse anesthetist. In the room, the radio is usually on, unless an operator specifically asks for no background music (as it easily happens in the neurosurgery operating room). At the moment the anesthesiologist begins induction and the patient begins to fall asleep, the anesthesiologist brings the Ambu mask close to the patient's mouth and proceeds with manual ventilation until the patient is completely asleep. The nurse anesthetist, meanwhile, takes the aspirator and the laryngoscope needed for intubation from the ventilator cart. The nurse anesthetist stops manual ventilation and intubates the patient; immediately afterward, s/he connects the tube to the ventilator arranged at the head of the bed. At this point, the nurse anesthetist usually fills out the anesthesiology chart, while the anesthesiologist leaves the operating room: sometimes s/he goes to get coffee, sometimes s/he stops to talk with colleagues in the hallway (and sometimes both).

If the surgeons are already in the room before the intubation phase, they wait standing beside the operating table for the patient to be anesthetized and covered with sterile drapes by the instrument nurse. It may also happen, however, that the operating room is reached first by one surgeon (usually the less experienced one) who starts disinfecting the operating field, and the other (the more experienced one) makes his or her appearance after a few minutes, or when the patient has already been "opened."

When both surgeons are in the operating room, they position them-selves on the left and right side of the operating table: one of them (the less experienced one) begins disinfecting the surgical field, while the other observes her/his colleague, often exchanging small talks with her/him about the surgery. Once the area of the body to be operated on has been disinfected, the instrument nurse hands the sterile drapes to the two sur-geons (which cover the patient's entire body, except for the surgical area) and approaches the table with the sterile irons to the foot of the operating table. If the surgery is of short duration, it is possible that, after just a few minutes, the nurse anesthetist asks the room staff nurse to fetch the next patient.

In the meantime, the nurse anesthetist continues the completion of the anesthesia chart and checks that the parameters monitored by the machine are in a normal range. The room staff nurse remains in the room, and while waiting for the instrument nurse to ask to handing some needles or instruments, s/he reads a magazine, or chats by the room door (which in most of the cases remains open) with the room staff nurse working in the sterilization room.

During the intervention, brief verbal interactions directly related to the work being done in the operating room take place between:

- the two surgeons, when the more experienced one asks his colleague to suction or hold open the surgical field;
- the instrument nurse and the experienced surgeon, when the latter asks for an instrument;
- the instrument nurse and the room staff nurse, when the instrument nurse asks the room staff nurse to take material and/or at the time of counting the gauzes;
- the nurse anesthetist and the anesthesiologist, when exchanging views about the patient's condition and about whether to administer a different dose of medication than is usually expected;
- one of the two surgeons and the room staff nurse, when the position of the operating light has to be changed.

It can also happen, however, that during the course of the surgery ten-sions arise between the experienced surgeon and the other operators in the room. Often, the more experienced surgeon will speak in ungentlemanly tones toward the room staff nurse (e.g., if the operating light is not properly positioned), or toward the instrumentist (if she does not work "ahead" and with the speed the surgeon would like).

It may also happen that one or more operators from outside the surgical team enter the room to talk to somebody of the team about surgeries scheduled for the following days, future holidays, or simply to ask for confirmation or denial of some rumors.

During the intervention, the patient may move and/or one of the two surgeons may feel the patient heavily contracting muscles. In the event that the anesthesiologist is not present in the room, the nurse anesthetist (usually sitting on the stool next to the ventilator) gets up, walks over to the medication cart, takes a syringe, and injects its contents in the drip inserted into the patient's arm. Then, s/he looks at the monitor and goes back sitting next to the ventilator.

When the anesthesiologist re-enters the operating room, the nurse tells him that more medication had to be administered because the patient was waking up. The anesthesiologist usually nods and sits beside the ventilator, checking that the nurse to took note of it on the anesthesiology chart.

Once the most challenging part of the surgery is over, the 'experienced' surgeon leaves the room, while the other 'closes' the operating field. At about the same time, the instrumentist asks the room staff nurse to count the gauzes. If the count is correct, the surgeon proceeds to close the surgical field; if the count is not correct, gauzes are counted one more time, and if the counts still do not add up, the surgeon present in the room asks the room staff nurse to communicate it to the surgeon who has just left. In the meantime, the surgeon in the room will either look in the patient's body for the gauze, or ask for an x-ray (in case the surgical field has already been closed).

At this stage, the anesthesiologist and instrument nurse remove the sterile drapes from the patient's body. The anesthesiologist interrupts the induction, and the second surgeon, having finished the suturing, approaches the small table on which is placed the chart relating to the treatment plan and begins to write down the type of surgery performed and the therapy to be given to the patient. The room staff nurse throws the used gauze into a black bag and checks the cart for sharps (which can happen), then closes the garbage bags, and takes them to the hallway, while the instrument nurse removes the drapes from the patient's body, cleans the surgical area, bandages the wound, and places a plaster on the operated part.

The patient starts waking up and the anesthesiologist proceeds with extubating while the nurse anesthetist takes the aspirator from the ventilator cart. After a few minutes, once extubated, the anesthesiologist speaks to the patient, reassuring him or her that it is all over and everything went well. After a few minutes of monitoring in the room, the anesthesiologist says that the patient can be moved to the corridor between the room and the preoperative area, where s/he will continue to be monitored. If the patient is already able to move, the room staff nurse (together with the nurse anesthetist) will help him/her to move from the bed to the stretcher; otherwise, the room staff nurse and the nurse anesthetist will ask the instrument nurse (and if necessary, also to the anesthesiologist) to help them move the patient from the bed to the stretcher. Having placed the patient on the stretcher, the room staff nurse takes the patient to the corridor separating the room from the preoperative area. The surgeons, meanwhile, are in front of the computer located at the end of the corridor, writing down the postoperative treatment plan.

The nurse anesthetist connects the patient to the pressure-monitoring machine and asks him if and how much pain s/he feels. The patient usually responds that s/he feels no pain or that the pain is bearable (with values ranging from 0 to 3); if not, the nurse anesthetist informs the anesthesiologist, who authorizes the nurse to administer a pain reliever.

After a few minutes of monitoring, the patient is transported back to the ward.

3.6.1   Surgerying: Technical Objects, Communication, and Professional Visions

The typified description of a surgery immediately highlights the prevalence habits and routines have over norms and protocols in orienting operators' daily actions. Emphasizing this aspect does not mean to claim that work practices are disconnected from protocols and guidelines, but to highlight the nonlinearity of this relationship. Bearing this in mind, we can therefore notice how the daily activity in the operating room is characterized by several factors:

– it is an activity articulated through various technologies, tools, and objects, which thus constitute the material infrastructure on which daily organizational and work practices rest and whose proper func-

tioning constitutes one of the *sine qua non* conditions for the realization of the work and organization in the operating block;
- it is an activity articulated between routine and improvisation, where the ability of operators to maintain a widespread attention to the work performed by colleagues and a constant communication about what is happening in the room is simply taken for granted;
- it is an activity articulated through different professional skills and visions, which are therefore called upon to interact and coordinate in order to ensure the proper management of the surgery.

In order to highlight how through technologies, communication-related practices, and professional knowledge the sociomateriality of medical practices emerges, we will now go into the details of the research.

REFERENCES

Agar, M. (1980). *The Professional Stranger*. Academic Press.
Atkinson, P. (1990). *The Ethnographic Imagination. Textual Construction of Reality*. Routledge.
Barad, K. (2003). Posthumanist Performativity: Toward an Understanding of How Matter Comes to Matter. *Signs, 28*(3), 801–831.
Barad, K. (2007). *Meeting the universe halfway: Quantum physics and the entanglement of mat-ter and meaning*. Durham and London, Duke University Press.
Barley, S., & Kunda, G. (2001). Bringing Work Back In. *Organization Science, 1*, 76–95.
Barley, S., & Kunda, G. (2004). *Gurus, Hired Guns and Warm Bodies*. Princeton University Press.
Bruni, A. (2005). Shadowing Software and Clinical Records: On the Ethnography of Non-Humans and Heterogeneous Contexts. *Organization, 12*, 357–378.
Bruni, A. (2010). *La sicurezza organizzativa. Una etnografia in sala operatoria*. Carocci.
Bruni, A., & Gherardi, S. (2001). Omega's Story: The Heterogeneous Engineering of a Gendered Professional Self. In M. Dent & S. Whitehead (Eds.), *Managing Professional Identities. Knowledge, Performativity and the New Professional*. Routledge.
Bruni, A., Gherardi, S., & Poggio, B. (2005). *Gender and Entrepreneurship: An Ethnographic Approach*. Routledge.
Burgess, R. G. (1988). *Studies in Qualitative Methodology*. JAI Press.
Callon, M. (1986). The Sociology of an Actor-Network: The Case of the Electric Vehicle. In M. Callon, J. Law, & A. Rip (Eds.), *Mapping the Dynamics of Science and Technology* (pp. 19–34). Palgrave Macmillan.

Clifford, J. (1983). On Ethnographic Authority. *Representations*, *1*, 118–146. (Repr. in *Qualitative Research*, ed. A. Bryman and R.G. Burgess. London: Sage, 1999).

Cooper, R., & Law, J. (1995). Distal and Proximal Visions of Organization. In S. Bacharach, P. Gagliardi, & B. Mundell (Eds.), *Studies of Organizations in the European Tradition* (pp. 237–274). Jai Press.

Czarniawska, B. (2004). On Time, Space and Action Nets. *Organization*, *11*, 777–795.

Czarniawska, B. (2007). *Shadowing and Other Techniques for Doing Fieldwork in Modern Societies*. Copenhagen Business School Press.

Czarniawska, B. (2014). Why I Think Shadowing is the Best Field Technique in Management and Organization Studies. *Qualitative Research in Organization and Management*, *9*(1), 90–93.

Engeström, Y., & Blackler, F. (2005). On the Life of the Object. *Organization*, *12*, 307–330.

Engeström, Y., & Middleton, D. (Eds.). (1996). *Cognition and Communication at Work*. Cambridge University Press.

Gagliardi, P. (Ed.). (1986). *Le imprese come culture*. ISEDI.

Garfinkel, H. (1967). *Studies in Ethnomethodology*. Prentice-Hall.

Geertz, C. (1973). *The Interpretation of Cultures*. Basic Books.

Gherardi, S. (2006). *Organizational Knowledge: The Texture of Workplace Learning*. Oxford, Blackwell.

Gherardi, S. (1990). *Le microdecisioni nelle organizzazioni*. il Mulino.

Gherardi, S. (2017). Sociomateriality in Posthuman Practice Theory. In S. Hui, E. Shove, & T. Schatzki (Eds.), *The Nexus of Practices: Connections, Constellations, and Practitioners* (pp. 38–51). Routledge.

Gill, R., Barbour, J. B., & Dean, M. (2014). Shadowing in/as Work: Ten Recommendations for Shadowing Fieldwork Practice. *Qualitative Research in Organizations and Management*, *9*(1).

Hammersley, M., & Atkinson, P. (1995). *Ethnography*. Routledge.

Hatch, M. J. (2019). *Organization Theory: Modern, Symbolic, and Postmodern Perspectives* (4th ed.). Oxford, Oxford University Press.

Heritage, J. (1984). *Garfinkel and Ethnomethodology*. Polity Press.

Knoblauch, H. (2005). Focused Ethnography. In *Forum Qualitative Social Research 6*(3). Retrieved from http://www.qualitative-research.net/index.php/fqs/article/view/20

Kunda, G. (1992). *Engineering Culture. Control and Commitment in a High-Tech Corporation*. Philadelphia, Temple University Press.

Latour, B. (2005). *Reassembling the Social. An Introduction to Actor-Network Theory*. Oxford University Press.

Lave, J., & Wenger, E. (1991). *Situated Learning. Legitimate Peripheral Participation*. Cambridge University Press.

Law, J. (2004). *After Method*. Routledge.

Manning, P. K. (1992). *Organizational Communication*. New York, Aldine de Gruyter.

Manning, P. K. (1995). The Challenges of Postmodernism. In J. Van Maanen (Ed.), *Representation in Ethnography*. Sage. (Repr. in A. Bryman and R.G. Burgess (eds), Qualitative Research, London, Sage, 1999).

Marcus, G. E., & Cushman, D. (1982). Ethnographies as Texts. *Annual Review of Anthropology, 11*, 25–69.

Martin, J. (1992). *Cultures in Organizations: Three Perspectives*. Oxford, Oxford University Press.

Mintzberg, H. (1973). *The Nature of Managerial Work*. Harper and Row.

Mol, A. (2002). *The Body Multiple: Ontology in Medical Practice*. Duke University Press.

Nicolini, D. (2009). Articulating Practice Through the Interview to the Double. *Management Learning, 40*(2), 195–212.

Niemimaa, M. (2014). Sociomaterial Ethnography: Taking the Matter Seriously. *MCIS Proceedings*.

Sachs, P. (1993). Shadows in the Soup: Conceptions of Work and Nature of Evidence. *Quarterly Newsletter of the Laboratory of Human Cognition, 15*, 125–132.

Schatzki, T. R., Knorr-Cetina, K., & von Savigny, E. (Eds.). (2001). *The Practice Turn in Contemporary Theory*. Routledge.

Schultze, U. (2011). The Avatar as Sociomaterial Entanglement: A Performative Perspective on Identity, Agency and World-Making in Virtual Worlds. In *International Conference of Information Systems*, Shangai.

Schütz, A. (1932). *Der Sinhafte Aufbau der Sozialen Welt*, transl. *The Phenomenology of the Social World*. Chicago: Northwestern University Press, 1967.

Schwartz, H., & Jacobs, J. (1979). *Qualitative Sociology: A Method to the Madness*. The Free Press.

Sclavi, M. (1989). *A una spanna da terra*. Feltrinelli.

Silverman, D. (1997). *Doing Qualitative Research*. Sage.

Strati, A. (1992). Aesthetic Understanding of Organizational Life. *The Academy of Management Review, 17*, 568–581.

Strati, A. (1996). *Sociologia dell'organizzazione*. Carocci.

Strati, A. (1999). *Organization and Aesthetics*. Sage.

Vasquez, C., Brummans, B. H. J. M., & Groleau, C. (2012). Notes from the Field on Organizational Shadowing as Framing. *Qualitative Research in Organizations and Management, 7*(2), 144–165.

Weick, K. (1976). Organizations as Loosely Coupled Systems. *Administrative Science Quarterly, 21*, 1–19.

CHAPTER 4

Working in the Operating Room, Flirting with Objects and Technologies

Abstract This chapter focuses on the array of technologies and technical objects within an operating unit, showing their essential role in the performance of everyday activities, and thus how organizational and work practices 'materialize' through different artifacts and technologies. From an interpretative point of view, the chapter proposes the metaphor of 'flirtation' to catch one of the main characteristics of everyday work in the operating room. That is, the unpredictable yet intimate relationship that arises between actors and technical objects in the operating room.

Finally, the chapter makes a point regarding the presence, the use, and the interferences of two 'mundane' technologies common to find in the operating room and which served as a background to the flow of activities: the radio and the smartphone.

Keywords Objects and technologies • Material infrastructure • Flirt • Mundane technologies

4.1 Devices of Everyday Work

An operating room can be straightforwardly seen as a technologically dense environment (Bruni, 2005; Bruni et al., 2013) in which heterogeneous practices mobilize the joint action of human and nonhuman actors.

© The Author(s), under exclusive license to Springer Nature Switzerland AG 2023
A. Bruni, *Sociomaterial Practices in Medical Work*,
https://doi.org/10.1007/978-3-031-44804-1_4

The array of technologies and technical objects within an operating unit is extremely broad and composite (safety devices, sanitary equipment, and machinery for the monitoring and life support of patients), and it is essential for the performance of everyday activities. Thus, we are facing an environment where human interactions and technological devices are mutually supportive for the smooth flow of collective work. In other words, an environment where the flow of daily activities requires human subjects and technological objects to work and "get along" together.

There are various intuitive examples of this "working together" of humans and technologies in the operating room: equipment and technical objects are a *sine qua non* for surgery, as witnessed also by the presence of an "instrument nurse" whose role consists precisely in making immediately available to the surgeon the instruments s/he needs to proceed with the operation. Beginning with the scalpel (without which the surgeon would not be able to cut the patient's body), continuing with the anesthesia drugs, mechanical ventilator, and endotracheal tube (without which it would not be possible to anesthetize and intubate the patient), up to the "gauzes count" (which marks the conclusion of the operation and consists of verifying that no gauze has been forgotten in the patient's body), instruments and technologies constantly accompany the surgical activity. Importantly, objects and technologies capturing actors' attention do not emerge because of their technical complexity, but because of their implications for the daily work.

In the variety of tools and technologies that operators refer to, personal protection equipment (PPE) is one of the most obvious examples. Shoe covers, headgear, gowns, masks, gloves, and (if necessary) protective eyewear are the technical items that transversally involve all operators and that, if not worn, prevent entry to the operating block. In other words, these are the technical objects that longest and most closely associate with actors' bodies and activities in the room. At the same time, despite their apparent technical simplicity, these objects are the result of complex sociotechnical networks, involving the action of biomedical companies and regulatory agencies, as well as of the individual organization that purchases and adopts them. This is to make explicit how (like many other objects and technologies) PPE represents the product of a network of sociomaterial practices that goes far beyond the walls of the organization in which they are situated, as well as a visible trace of the sociomaterial dimension of the processes and practices that take shape in the operating room.

This sociomaterial dimension is also reflected in the different ways different occupational groups approached and used PPEs. A case in point is the use of gloves. As reported by an instrument nurse still in training, his colleagues taught him to wear two pairs of gloves (one on top of the other) because: "The first is a medical device, while the second is a personal protective equipment." It should be noted that, because of the type of activities in which they are involved, instrument nurses spend most of their time in the operating room and (along with surgeons) are most likely to come into contact with patients' blood. As made explicit by the commentary quoted just above, therefore, gloves are a useful material ally for this community of actors in order to limit the risks associated with daily work. And since these risks affect operators but also patients, two pairs of gloves are worn, in their dual capacity of "medical device" (thus aimed at patient safety) and "personal protective equipment" (aimed at the safety of the individual operator).

Among surgeons and anesthesiologists, on the contrary, the use of gloves is limited to one pair and becomes a matter of open discussion in the case of latex-free gloves. A specific protocol recommends that in case of emergencies (therefore regarding patients to whom no questions can be asked because they are unconscious), gloves made of synthetic polymers should be used to prevent the risk of allergies in patients. However, some surgeons (especially in neurosurgery, where smaller instruments are used) refuse to wear them, arguing that these do not allow the same sensitivity given by latex ones. A similar controversy develops around the use of face masks and goggles: according to some surgeons, face mask and goggles "don't get along," in the sense that the former causes the latter to fog up, so it is also possible for the surgeon to begin an operation wearing both goggles and face mask, but ending only with the face mask alone. Furthermore, in neurosurgery, several surgeons ask to be allowed to operate barefoot, since (they say) shoes and shoe covers complicate being able to find and maintain the body balance necessary to perform the micro-movements that characterize neurological surgeries.

All together, these examples highlight how PPEs become "safe" or "risky" depending on the practices they are inserted in. This shifting nature of PPEs testifies their ontological multiplicity: as for the gloves, their properties change in relation to the actors, the performances, and the other materials they meet. The sociomaterial articulation of organizational action depends not only on the relationships between humans and objects (as in the case of latex-free gloves and barefoot operation), but also between objects and objects (as in the case of the face mask and protective goggles), and between humans and humans (as in the case of the learning trajectory of instrumentalists). A sociomaterial reading of organization and work, in fact, does not locate 'social' properties and capacities in humans and 'material' ones in objects and technologies, but strives to emphasize the different degrees (Cooren, 2020) by which social and material manifest and blur each other. The examples just seen show the continuous recurrences (rather than demarcation) between humans and objects, as well as the materiality of human action (insofar as it involves the body), the sociality of objects (insofar as they associate with other objects), and the material constraints the human body poses for the associations between objects.

Moreover, the fact that PPEs are sometimes perceived as a management imposition that does not take into account the real needs and difficulties of everyday work, makes their observance becoming in some cases almost a matter of challenge. As from the words of one surgeon: "Wearing mask or gloves it's my own damn business! Also because unless there's somebody in the room telling you: 'Put your cap on!', I mean... once in a while there is ... but still, the assumption is that we're all of legal age, so ...."

These kinds of statements and attitudes reflect a well-known organizational dynamic: sometimes operators take safety procedures as an inadmissible intrusion within their professional and personal autonomy. Not surprisingly, within the observations protagonists of these situations and expressions are almost always surgeons and/or anesthesiologists, undoubtedly the two professional categories that in an operating team enjoy greater autonomy and are therefore less accustomed to having to negotiate the performance of their work. In this sense, it should be made explicit how asymmetries of status and power are also reflected in the use of instruments and devices. As stated by the above surgeon, almost no one calls out colleagues on their behaviors regarding the use of PPEs, and in fact during the observations, it was rather immediate to note that only a few experienced instrument nurses could "reprimand" (often through the exercise of irony) anesthesiologists and/or surgeons not properly wearing PPEs.

This does not justify the systematic inattentions that some practitioners had toward PPEs, but it recalls attention to how objects and technologies should be read and evaluated in relation not only to their technical functionalities but in reference to the broader uses and meanings they acquire in their use, they trigger in their users, and by the way they intersect with a broader set of organizational practices and dynamics. That is, in relation to their sociomaterial dimensions.

4.2 FLIRTING WITH MATERIALITY, PERFORMING ORGANIZATION

Looking at personal protection equipment, we began to sketch the ways humans and technical objects co-construct ordinary working practices in the operating room. Focusing on some specific episodes, we will now see how PPEs, tools, and technologies of diverse technical complexity form the material infrastructure on which organizing and work practices in the operating room rest. As famously noted by Star (1999), infrastructures are mostly taken for granted, but they acquire visibility in occasions of breakdown. Thus, in order to show the material infrastructure of everyday work, the following three episodes of momentary breakdown in the operating room will be illustrated:

1. when a technical object in everyday use changes;
2. when a technical object in everyday use breaks;
3. when a technical object in everyday use is absent.

We shall see how each of these situations activates (and makes necessary) a search for a new alignment between the performance of activities and the material elements present. We shall also see how such situations enact what can be metaphorically interpreted as a kind of 'flirtation' between actors and the material world. In sociology, Georg Simmel (1908) was the first to approach flirtation as a distinct form of interaction, defining it "a promise without a guarantee," an "enticing gamble" (p. 143), "the ability and inability to acquire something" (Simmel, 1984, p. 134). For Simmel, flirtation represents a game of possibilities (Pinsky, 2019), and as such, it belongs to a larger class of "suspended interactions" where participants manage different interactional frames (Goffman, 1974) in order to leave the unfolding of the situation open. From this point of view, flirtation is an interactional form in which ambiguity itself is the object of interaction (Tavory, 2009). At the level of interaction, flirting often implies a combination of gestures and talk characterized by elusiveness and deniability so that it can be difficult to definitively identify a behavior as flirtation (Kozin, 2016; Speer, 2017). Flirting implies the existence of multiple possible interpretations of the same action (Kiesling, 2013: 106), so that "it may be characteristic of flirting that it is 'designedly' ambiguous and hence not meant to be pinned down" (Speer, 2017: 5).

The scant academic research on flirtation has conceptualized the act of flirting as an interaction between humans, although nowadays widely intertwined with the use of social media and digital platforms for online encounters (Pinsky, 2019). In what follows I shall use the metaphor of 'flirtation' as a construct with which to interpret and increase the understanding of the sociomaterial dimension of work and organizing practices, stressing the intimate relationship, but never with entirely predictable outcomes, that ties together actors, technologies, and the material world.

4.3   When a Technical Object Changes: Flirting with the New Cannula Needles

In the operating room, it is 7.25 when Anna, nurse anesthetist, reads the operating list. She checks the machine monitoring the life parameters and the one providing the patient's controlled ventilation. As she checks the proper functioning of these devices, Anna joins the preoperative area in order to prepare the phleboclysis for all the operations scheduled during the morning session. She says that, from today, new cannula needles will be used for a trial period: "These are needles with a particular security mechanism that should guarantee us nurses and the patients more than before." Then she adds: "I've never tried them."

Anna opens a drawer (where cannula needles are usually put) and realizes there are no old models, just new ones. She takes one of them and figures out how it works. She triggers the spring inside the needle so as to verify the click and therefore understand how to apply it to the patients; in so doing, she looks more confident and asks a nurse to call the first patient scheduled for the day.

After a few minutes, the patient enters the preoperative area, carried on a stretcher by the nurse. As Anna takes everything necessary to plug the phleboclysis into the patient's arm, Anna says to the latter: "Today is the first time I've used these needles, so…let's hope everything goes well!" The patient does not look worried and smiles at her. Anna plugs in the phleboclysis. But as she presses the button triggering the spring inside the needle, a large amount of blood spurts from the patient's vein. There is blood on the patient's arm, on the arm of the nurse, and on most of the sheet covering the patient.

Anna is not wearing gloves. She takes the cotton wool she has used to disinfect the part of the arm where the phleboclysis is to be inserted and applies pressure to stop the flow of blood. When the flow has stopped, she runs to wash her hands, puts on the gloves, and then cleans the patient's hand and arm with some more cotton wool. The instrument nurse, who is in the operating room, realizes that something is going wrong and comes to the lobby. Anna explains to her what has happened, and the instrument nurse replies: "*Report it! What's the point in sending them [the new needles] to be safer and then you get dirty like in Shining….*" However, Anna feels that she only needs to get used to the new needles and says: "*Perhaps it was my fault.*" Anna takes off the gloves and puts new ones on, although she points out: "*With the gloves I have less manual sensitivity.*" The second attempt, however, is successful and the phleboclysis is inserted.

In this episode, we see how a technical object introduced by the organization in order to ensure the safety of operators and patients (the new model of cannula needle) suddenly becomes a risky instrument for all the actors involved in the situation, as the nurse anesthetist was not skilled in its use. This highlights the role and the importance of tacit knowledge (Polanyi, 1958) in working practices and the ways in which technologies and work practices depend upon these sorts of skills. As aptly noted by Pinch (2008: 466) in reference to the institutional dimension of skills: "An organization like a hospital can only function because the doctors and nurses possess the bodily skills to carry out surgical operations, make other medical interventions, and care for patients."

As stressed by various authors, the tools and technologies typical of an activity come almost to constitute prostheses (Stone, 1995) of the practitioners' bodies, so that even an expert nurse may find herself in difficulty when facing a cannula needle she has never previously used. The putting into use and translation into work practice of instruments and technologies is indeed dependent on the technical characteristics of the objects, but these same characteristics assume concreteness only in relation to different subjects and activities. Once again, objects' characteristics emerge through a joint consideration of the technical features and social practice they build upon. This consideration also makes it possible to interpret from a standpoint alternative to the procedural one the fact that the anesthetist nurse was not wearing protective gloves. This is indubitably a breach of organizational safety rules, but from the point of view of the anesthetist nurse, gloves reduce touch and sensitivity, so that it is preferable to work barehanded if one wants to immediately find the patient's vein.

In other words, a shift in one of the elements involved in the material infrastructure of everyday work (the phleboclysis) causes a momentary lapse of practice in a routinized clinical action (finding the patient's vein). The matching between new cannula needles and organizational safety standards displaces the positive flirt the anesthetist nurse used to have with previous cannula needles, so that her colleague suggests reporting the 'betray' of the new needles (which, on the contrary, promised to be more reliable). The body knowledge of the nurse suddenly vanishes, making evident the importance of another technical object (the gloves) that should be part of the relationship, but with which the nurse does not have a positive flirt.

A second consideration concerns the construction of organizational action: the above episode shows that what happens in the operating room is closely connected to practices and events occurring in different organizational times and spaces. The choice of the new needles had been made at a time and in a place separate from those in which the action takes place. Actors were informed about the introduction of the new needles for a trial period, but they were not aware this would have implied the complete elimination of those previously in use, another decision taken by the management in a different time and place which reverberates on the situation. This directs attention to the action net that arises around humans and technologies, and to the kairotic dimension of organizational decisions and action (Czarniawska, 2004).

The episode highlights the complex web of sociomaterial relations that tie technological objects and actors together, highlighting at the same time the material infrastructure on which everyday activities are based and the flirtations actors have with it. To continue along this trajectory, now presented is a situation in which an instrument essential for the performance of surgical operations stops working, triggering a series of sociomaterial flirts intended to remedy the breakdown and conclude the surgery.

4.4   WHEN A TECHNICAL OBJECT BREAKS: FLIRTING WITH THE MICROSCOPE

The operation is performed with the aid of a microscope and a monitor (on which images of the operation are projected). The room staff nurse turns off the lights in the room and positions the microscope following the surgeon's instructions. Sitting to the left of the patient is the surgeon, standing to the right of the operating table is the instrument nurse, while the nurse anesthetist (Giada) and the anesthesiologist (Chiara) sit on two stools against the wall.

Suddenly, the microscope goes dark. "The bulb needs changing," the instrument nurse says. There is general agitation. The instrument nurse tries to remove the flap on the microscope to change the bulb, but in vain: the flap is jammed. The instrument nurse asks the room staff nurse to call someone from the next-door operating room. The room staff nurse returns after some seconds, saying: "He wanted to come, but the consultant stopped him, saying that we must sort it out by ourselves." The instrument nurse: "But it's not our fault! And... did you tell him we're operating? Anyway, call the clinical engineer and tell him to send someone immediately. Immediately!" In the meantime, she keeps trying to remove the flap. Chiara and Giada try to help her, but without success. The instrument nurse from the next-door operating room arrives. After a couple of minutes, he manages to open the flap and to change the bulb.

As it usually happens in occasion of breakdowns, infrastructures emerge (Star, 1999). In our particular case, as from the episode above, the material infrastructure of everyday work is particularly 'large' (the operating room is simply full of instruments, cables, devices, and technologies) so that a sort of 'technological stratification' takes place. Even though in the operating room the majority of objects and technologies is largely taken for granted in their being 'naturally' part of the activities, some of them are more 'invisible' than others, either because of their material visibility (a personal safety device or a scalpel is much more visible than a light bulb 'hidden' into a microscope), either because of their technical stability and durability (the more an object or a technology does not break or require maintenance, the more it will be likely to disappear in the eye of the practitioners). The microscope and the light bulb, in fact, become 'visible' only after the breakdown: as long as the light bulb was working, it was 'transparent,' part of the microscope. This makes explicit how everyday work relies on a plurality of technical objects, often interconnected, and which may turn into infrastructural elements for each other. In an ecological approach to technologies, in fact, that of 'infrastructure' is a relational concept (Star, 1999), since what for some is taken for granted, for others is the object of the activity. But an infrastructure is 'relational' also from a technical and material point of view, since its stability and durability are embedded in an extensive network of interconnected technological artifacts (the image on the monitor appears because of the microscope, which in turn implies the light bulb, and so on).

From a sociomaterial point of view, organizational structures and infrastructures are always related (Plesner & Husted, 2019), and in fact in our episode in front of a breakdown of the material infrastructure, the social and organizational structures emerge. The social structure is that of the community of practice the instrument nurse is part of, as she tries to call into action a more expert colleague. The organizational structure is mirrored in the chief consultant "stopping" the instrument nurse and not allowing him to help in the next-door operating room, and in the instrument nurse asking for the maintenance technicians once informed of the reaction of the chief consultant.

From a metaphorical point of view, the instrument nurse tries to solve the technical breakdown by a series of quick material flirtations: first with the microscope, trying to change the light bulb (but the flap is jammed); and then with the architectures, looking in the operating room next door for a more expert colleague (whom, by the way, is "stopped" by the chief consultant). Thus, flirting with the material world actors realize the constraints imposed by the structural and infrastructural relations and interactions among objects, as well as among actors themselves.

In this regard, it is of interest to consider what happens in the absence of a technical object necessary for the operation to be properly performed.

4.5   When a Technical Object Is Missing: Flirting with the Material World

The instrument nurse (Sofia) tells the nurse anesthetist (Giulia): "We've only got three pairs of goggles, so you've got to stay outside."

The surgery will be performed using a laser, so that all those present in the room must wear protective goggles. But there are five operators: the surgeon, the instrument nurse, the room staff nurse, the anesthetist, and Giulia. So it is decided that Giulia will remain outside the room and that the room staff nurse will turn to face the wall when the laser is being used.

In this short episode, the absence of a device for individual protection (the protective goggles) triggers a series of improvised organizational dynamics. The decision to have an operator (the nurse anesthetist) leaving the room, and to ask another (the room staff nurse) to turn to the wall (while the laser was being used), can be interpreted as a repair practice intended to align (and to have coincide) the human and artificial elements present in the operating room. As often happens in the case of repair practices, the ability to improvise is crucial—confirming that work (in the operating room, but not only there) can be interpreted as akin to a performance constructed by moving in space among diverse materials.

The episode exemplifies the rapidity and the naturalness with which actors orient themselves among the different affordances offered by the physical world as they search for some sort of complicity from the objects (and, in our case, the architectures) present on the scene. As if flirting with the material elements present in the operating room, the actors searched the environment around them for action resources and, in this particular case, made up for the absence of the protective goggles by reconfiguring (in number and position) the actors present in the operating room. From this point of view, flirting with the material world can be interpreted in terms of a performance which requires an improvised choreography (Whalen et al., 2002) of human and nonhuman elements. The situation described (like the 'choreographic' solution adopted) is evidently at odds with organizational protocols and rules; but is the misalignment among the rules, activities, and materials to enacting the actors' deviation from routine trajectories and, at the same time, orienting action to the reconstruction of a sufficiently safe work context.

In sociomaterial terms, and perhaps somewhat paradoxically, this episode shows how the diverse professional competencies present during an operating session are also defined in relation to objects. Some technical objects (such as the surgical instruments) are of exclusive competence of surgeons and instrument nurses; others (for instance, the apparatus for monitoring the vital functions of patients) are the responsibility of anesthesiologists and nurse anesthetists; yet others (typically, gauzes, and soiled materials) are the concern of the room staff nurse. Hence, the decision on who should leave the operating room is also determined by the various 'technical worlds' with which organizational actors interrelate. To be noted is that in the above extract two pairs of goggles are lacking, but only the nurse anesthetist is asked to leave the room. If the presence of the anesthesiologist is sufficient to maintain stable relationships with the technical world of anesthesia, neither the surgeon nor the instrument nurse would be able to deal with the technical world of the room staff nurse (also because room staff nurses come into contact with numerous nonsterile objects). From a sociomaterial perspective, therefore, the exclusion of the nurse anesthetist from the operating room is due not only to the absence of a pair of goggles but also to the lack for this particular figure of an 'exclusive' relationship with a particular technical world.

Finally, this episode gives the occasion to underline the relationship and the difference between the idea of 'flirting' and the concept of affordance. For Gibson (1979), affordances are properties of the material world which may be picked up by actors in order to pursue their objectives; or, which may suggest possibilities of action a subject did not consider before. The materiality of the world is an 'invitation to,' an 'occasion for,' a repertoire of actions. Affordances direct the attention of actors to some of the possibilities offered by the environment, but at the same time, they depend on the actor's interests and the capacity for action. Moreover, affordances can be nested or grouped, when the possibility of action is articulated in more hierarchically ordered sub-actions (as in the case of the affordance of 'pulling' a door handle, which is nested in that of 'opening' the door—Gaver, 1991). This 'sequential' property of affordances directs attention to the idea that some affordances will be present only at a certain stage of action and that 'exploration' is a key dimension of being-in-the-world.

In my view, the idea of 'flirting' with the material world is precisely an attempt to focus on this exploration. Interpreting the relations between actors and the materiality of the world in terms of flirtation makes it possible to highlight not only that material settings present affordances but also how the relations between actors and the setting are constructed on a series of reciprocal interpellations, solicitations, and responses. In the above and previous episode, it becomes apparent how the flirtation of the actors with the physical world was constructed as a constant process that pervaded the entire activity and was not restricted to situations of explicit breakdown (like those considered thus far).

The next section will thus concentrate on some of the more ordinary working practices, the purpose being to shed further light on the interactions that arise between human actors and material world.

4.6   Flirting with Lists and Instruments, Articulating Everyday Work

In the operating room, the beginning of the day is marked by the reading of the list of scheduled operations. Consulting the list enables the personnel to imagine the day ahead and therefore to begin arranging the work:

After checking the list of operators present in the operating room today, the anesthesiologist walks down the corridor to the neurosurgery room. The anesthesiologist is used to check every morning who are the operators who will be working with her: "You have to check before you go to the room… because you understand who you are with and if maybe you will need a hand… or, like last week, if you have another anesthesiologist with you."

In material terms, the operating list is nothing more than a sheet of paper. However, as from the proposed excerpt, it represents an indispensable object for members of the surgical team to figure out the flow of the day. "Looking at the list" thus is not a practice directed at a numerical and/or functional verification of the operators present in the team, but above all at figuring out with whom one will share the work (as the anesthesiologist points out, by reading the list "you figure out who you are with"). The relatively small number of operators indeed facilitates their knowing each other, both in professional terms and from the point of view of interaction and character: some of them have a very high tone of voice, others are often nervous, while some others are appreciated for their sense of irony or (as we shall see later) for the music they bring to the operating room.

In addition, experience often leads actors to develop their own working style, whose knowledge enables operators to provide for a range of objects and prevent a number of issues:

Scheduled for today are four operations, all mastectomies. At 7.20 the room staff nurse (Franco) and the instrument nurse (Flavia) enter, flanked by a newly-hired instrument nurse (Lucio). Franco cleans the floor, while Lucio asks Flavia for information about the instruments to use and the physical positioning of the four patients. Flavia answers Lucio, shows him the containers of the instruments to use, and also tells him the sizes of the gloves that the surgeons present today in the room usually use. Franco turns on the radio and goes away. Flavia reassures Lucio: "You can easily do two breasts on your own. Those with quadrants are a bit more complicated because they need other instruments, but don't worry."

At 7.30, the nurse anesthetist (Matteo) enters the room, together with Marianna, an nurse anesthetist who has previously worked in the intensive care unit but will shortly be transferred to the operating room. After looking at the list of operations, Matteo tells Marianna: "They're all under general anaesthesia today." Matteo explains how the fan works to Marianna, the phases in preparation of the drugs, and the 'preferences' of the anaesthetist today in the room on the use of some drugs rather than others. Matteo tells Marianna that Doctor Giusti will be in the room today, and then adds: "The reinforced tube won't be necessary."

As from the above extracts, to each activity in the operating room corresponds a particular set of instruments, and also the difficulty of an operation is assessed in terms of the instrumentation involved (as in the words of the instrument nurse: "Those with quadrants are a bit more complicated because they need other instruments"). It is also significant that the instructions given to novices mainly concern instruments and their associations with some of the staff who will be present in the operating room. In this way, the most experienced staff directs the attention of the novices not only to the interweaving between technical objects and activity but also to the relations between humans and technological artifacts. The reading of the list thus makes it possible to activate what Steinhardt and Jackson (2015: 3) define as anticipation work, "the complex behaviors and practices that define, enact and maintain vision across individual and collective, and temporally close and distant scales." Anticipation work is crucial for building a shared future around which distributed actions can be calibrated and to assert: "the forms of knowledge and infrastructure that are of greatest importance, or the kinds of technical resources that will persist into future generations" (Steinhardt & Jackson, 2015: 8).

Moreover, in our case, anticipation work permits in its turn a peculiar kind of "articulation work" (Strauss et al., 1985). A key characteristic of articulation work is to modify action so to accommodate unanticipated contingencies: it is the type of work people perform to be able to cope with 'real-and-proper' work (Star, 1999). In its original definition (Strauss et al., 1985), it was mainly referred to the continuous activities and interactions among organizational actors oriented to keep aligned the various tasks required to be performed in medical work. Here, it is intended to fluidify the encounters between people and instruments, so that the technologies normally used (or better, "preferred") by certain practitioners are immediately available.

As noted by Star (1991: 275), articulation work "gets things back 'on track' in the face of the unexpected, and modifies action to accommodate unanticipated contingencies." Precisely because of this, facilitating the encounters between humans and technologies may also take to make changes to the list. For instance, if several operations of the same kind are scheduled, the surgeons may ask for them to be grouped together so that it is not necessary to alter the set-up of the operating table:

> During the second operating session, the room staff nurse, on the instructions of one of the two surgeons in the room, phones the ward to say to change the order of the list. "It's better to do the other hernia first, so the table is already set," the surgeon says.

Episodes such as the one just mentioned further demonstrate the intimate relationship that binds technical objects and the organization of daily work and allow to understand why, at the beginning of the day, in the operating block everybody is looking for "the list": "Have you seen the list?"; Have you got the list?; "Where is the list?"; "Is the list up to date?"; "Has the list been changed?"; and so on.

Not surprisingly, changes in the operating list may create extra work for other room staff, as in the following case:

> The room staff nurse (Daniela) is cleaning the instruments in the three containers placed on the counter in the sterilization room (adjoining the operating room), when the instrument nurse (Giada) comes in and tells her that the laser that has just been used is required for the next operation. Handing the instrument to Daniela, Giada adds that, because there are no other lasers, she must wash the one just used as quickly as possible. Giada walks out and Daniela says that at times like these absolute sterility cannot be guaranteed, because accelerating sterilization requires a rapid wash and not a complete cycle. She places the instrument in a container with warm water and detergent. She then takes a sponge and a toothbrush and begins to wash the instrument. After a few minutes of washing 'by hand', Daniela puts the laser in the sterilizer, adds some detergent, and starts the (short) sterilization cycle, on completion of which the laser is ready.

In situations like the one described, human action is geared to linking the times and action of machines with organizational plans and work practices. In sociomaterial terms, it is possible to discern in such situations the constitutive role machines have for work, and thus the need of maintaining aligned human and technical activities. In metaphorical terms, we can take this episode as an example of how in flirting with objects actors move between different interactional frames (which in this case I would call "sterilizing the instrument" and "washing the dishes"), so to strip these latter of their technical refinement and approach them as they were more ordinary objects. As such, instruments can be treated in more ordinary ways: the room staff nurse washes the laser by hand in order to 'off-set' the choice of a 'short' sterilization cycle (and return the laser in the time necessary), as people sometimes do at home before putting a particularly dirty plate in the dishwasher. Similarly, on other occasions, the instrument nurses dried the instruments to complete the work begun by the instrument washer:

> The instrument nurse (Giovanna) is in charge of checking and arranging the irons used by the different operating rooms throughout the morning. However, the irons are still wet, and Giovanna explains that this happens when using the old iron washer, which does not "blanch" the instruments: "There is only one iron washer left on this floor, and with the fact that you want to create the sterilization area down, you don't bother to have all the others, which are broken, repaired." Giovanna transports the containers to the sterilization room. Here the operators give to Giovanna five dirty irons to be re-washed, so Giovanna takes the irons and goes to the washing room to hand them over to the staff nurse. Then she takes the already washed irons and, in the hallway, fixes them with the help of Sofia, who says: "The light here is not the best to do this kind of operation, because you have to check for stains or scaling. You would need a special room for that. Here, however, in addition to there being no light, it's also a transit area because we are in front of the balcony and people come in and out to go smoke."

In this episode, as in the one presented earlier, the impossibility of guaranteeing the sterility of a technical object (a laser, scalpel, or other instrument) calls the actors to perform some (invisible) work to support the technology: when faced with the malfunction of an 'old' technology (the iron-washing machine), to prevent fouling, the instrument nurses hand-dry the irons and check firsthand the quality of the work performed by the machines. As explained by the instrument nurse, if the iron-washing machine does not "blanch" the irons, fouling may be created on them. Moreover, the poor light in the corridors does not help to detect such fouling, thus increasing the number of irons that appear to be clean, but which are judged dirty by the operators once they reach the room, and have to be washed again (an event which in the observations conducted occurred with some frequency). Once again, the human work is directed at reconciling the technical times of the machines (e.g., those related to the sterilization of instruments) with the rhythm of the activities, and it does so by moving between two different interactional frames, a more 'scientific' (the sterilization) and a more 'mundane' one (the hand-drying and eye-checking).

But the situations in which humans support technologies and objects are not just about washing irons, as from the episode to follow:

> Suddenly, there is a blackout in the operating block. An uninterruptible power supply powers the operating rooms, but not the Head nurse's office, whose computer shut down. The Head nurse goes to the rooms to warn that the power is out: "Check that the respirators are going!" but by the time she gets to the third room, the power is already back. The Head nurse then makes a phone call, asking to check that the boiler has not jammed, in which case technicians must be called to unblock it.

In the case just presented, the Head nurse not only connects the work of the technology with that of the operators (alerting the latter to the absence of power), but also anticipates the resolution of a possible problem (the blockage of a boiler) that, according to her experience, may occur as a result of a power failure.

We thus see emerging again the theme of the material infrastructure on which organizational processes and work practices rest: the iron-washing machine that does not dry perfectly, the nonsterile corridors in which instruments are passed, the light in the corridors that does not allow optimal visibility for checking the cleanliness of instruments, all qualify as infrastructural with respect to daily work and call actors to pay attention to the different technical objects of which the organization is made. Flirting with these same objects and technologies allows actors to dwelling with the inherent ambiguity of such interactions, and to incorporating it into their work and organizational practices.

4.7 Radios, Personal Computer, and Cell Phones: Flirting with Mundane Technologies

A further trace of the sociomaterial dimension of medical work can be found in two 'mundane' technologies which the practitioners brought into the operating room and which served as a background (or better, a sound track) to the flow of activities: the radio and the cell phone.[1]

---

[1] When the research was conducted, in 2010, smartphones had just been introduced on the market, so that the large majority of operators had a mobile phone. This is also why digital practices and technologies are basically absent from the description: at least in the observed context, they did not enter the activities yet.

Especially in the general surgery operating room the presence of the radio immediately stands out to the eyes and ears of an outside observer. The positive effect that listening to music can have on surgical staff and patients during an operation is widely documented in the medical literature (Ullman et al., 2008), but what I would like to emphasize here is how flirting with mundane technologies helps to recreate a sense of everyday life in the operating room, as in the case to follow:

> The first surgery of the day has begun, the radio is on, and the atmosphere in the operating room is relaxed, to the point that the anesthesiologist pulls a computer and two portable speakers out of his bag and engages in a series of electronic connections while commenting: "The quality of the music is always so low in this room that one has to organize a bit...." [...] During the operation, I notice that the instrument nurse sometimes detaches her eyes from the operating field to look instead at the anesthesiologist fiddling, ditto when activating the computer screen saver. This displays some photos taken by the anesthesiologist during his last holidays, and after a while a room staff nurse asks the anesthesiologist which country he went to. Thus, the anesthesiologist starts talking about his last trip and, together with the room staff nurse, spends a few minutes in commenting on the photos scrolling on the screen saver. [...] With the surgery almost completed, the surgeon lets her younger colleague finish suturing the wound; so she walks over to the computer to look at the anesthesiologist's music library and to choose a music she likes.

In the situation presented, the détente atmosphere is palpable: the work activity seems to move into the background to leave room for actors' attitudes and the possibility of expressing not only their roles but also their subjectivities. We are thus facing mundane interactions that allow actors to appropriate the work space, characterizing the organizational context through a series of elements (music) and recreating a sense of the place and of the activity.

At the same time, the appearance of a 'mundane' technology (the computer) attracts actors' attention beyond measure, and even its installation distracts some operators from the ordinary course of action. Like in other situations already considered, we can thus see the active role technologies and objects play in everyday organizational life, characterizing the environment in which they are situated, and attracting and stimulating actors' attention and curiosity. In the proposed excerpt, in fact, the instrument nurse, the staff nurse, and the surgeon are those most attracted by the computer, although they are not the ones who brought it into the room. Moreover, during the observations, it happened that, for instance, some personnel followed the lyrics of a song rather than the interactions ongoing in the operating room; or that a staff nurse was at a distance from the operating table at a crucial moment because the surgeon had asked for the radio station to be changed; or that an anesthetist did dance steps close to the tangle of cables connecting the patient to the life support apparatus. All these cases could be interpreted as evident misconducts in regard to organizational norms, but in a sociomaterial lens, they are fruitful indicators of the constant and reciprocal influences that tie actors, technologies, organizational, and mundane practices.

The case of the cell phone is different. Cell phones (even if private) helped the personnel handle unexpected events, emergencies, and just-in-time coordination. When the Head nurse started work in the morning, she frequently used her cell phone to contact staff who had not yet arrived. Again, with her cell phone, she could instantly verify the availability of the personnel in order to substitute absentees. Or, she could be easily reached by staff in emergencies.

Likewise, when surgeons and anesthesiologists were urgently needed, they were contacted through their cell phone numbers, rather than through the pagers provided by the organization. Far from being an intimate and private technology, the cell phone is immediately "put to work," becoming another technology on which organizational action relies. However, the presence of cell phones also meant that they might ring at a critical moment of the surgery (usually irritating the surgeon at work), or that (especially during routine surgeries) operators could concentrate on reading/sending text messages. Indeed, in some extreme cases, it was possible to observe surgeons and/or anesthesiologists interrupt the operation in progress and/or go out of the room to answer a call.

Thus, the presence of a mundane technology such as the cell phone could also constitute an additional and everyday interference in work practices, importing into the work space issues and relationships pertaining to the actors' private life and introducing moments of discontinuity within the activity. This once again brings attention back to the sociomaterial character of organizational action and invites to search in the various flirtations actors have with objects and technologies the nodes capable of giving stability to organizational practices. Although radios, PCs, and cell phones are the result of different sociomaterial networks (especially if we look at them historically—Balbi & Magaudda, 2018), they testify the broad spectrum of objects and technologies with which actors flirt. Flirting with radios, PCs, and cell phones, actors recreate a sense of mundanity (as in the case of the radio), skip organizational technologies and practices they have no feeling with (as in the case of the pagers provided by the organization), and alternate linkages between organizational coordination and ordinary communication (as in the case of cell phones).

In other occasions, actors were attracted by these mundane technologies either because of their affordances (as in situations when the practitioners paid more attention to the images displayed by the computer screen or to the private chats on their cell phones), or because of the aesthetic inducements (Strati, 1999) they addressed to them (as when someone was 'carried away' by the music from the radio), or because of their immediacy and availability (as in situations where practitioners used their cell phones to contact a colleague).

This highlights the relevance of the different material flirtations actors have at work and during their everyday life, and of alternating longstanding and routinized organizational relationships with quick and ambiguous interactions with objects and technologies. The purpose of the metaphor of 'flirtation' is in fact that of emphasizing the 'complicity,' and at the same time the occasionality and indeterminacy that characterize the relations between actors and the material world. Metaphorically, just as flirtation is based on a form of free interaction (Simmel, 1908) "extraneous to the patterns of interaction that immobilize men and women" (Turnaturi, 1994: 27), so encounters between actors and the material world sometimes follow unusual trajectories that require redefinition and recontextualization of roles, relations, and agency. And just as flirtation implies a certain type of indeterminacy as regards the outcome of interaction, so in relations between actors and artifacts, the material world 'opens up' to new kinds of action, interaction, and meaning, to the point that it "changes register" (Crouch, 2010: 5) in even its most usual forms.

Interpreting the sociomaterial relations, actors are kept in as 'flirtation' underlines that the essence of a specific work setting (like an operating room) resides not only in the situated knowledge that enables actors to hold the different 'pieces' of the work together, but also in the fact that these 'pieces' are practical accomplishments fueled by the encounter (in some cases temporary, in others more enduring) between actors, objects, and technologies. Different ethnographic episodes are united by the intimate relationship that develops between instruments and actors, and which is strengthened by the constant search by the latter for material elements that can develop into further resources for action. Moreover, we have seen that the flirtation of actors with the materiality of the world (like any other form of relationship) does not come about in an entirely 'free' manner. Rather, it is embedded in a repertoire of practices and in the constraints imposed by the structural and infrastructural interactions that take place among both actors and objects.

Finally, the metaphor of flirtation directs attention to the reciprocity that arises between actors and technological artifacts, and therefore to the empathetic, emotional, and aesthetic ways in which actors are 'captured' by material settings. An almost carnal understanding between the technical artifacts of the operating room and the bodies of the participants in the activity takes place, which reflexively requires the latter to respond to the 'material' solicitations to which they are exposed. If technology is a prosecution of society with other means (Latour, 1992), then it is through flirting with the diverse materials that populate the setting in which action takes place that actors are able to recompose and install a network of reciprocal relations (humans-humans; humans-objects; objects-objects) that substantiate and perform everyday work and organizational life.

REFERENCES

Balbi, G., & Magaudda, P. (2018). *A History of Digital Media. An Intermedia and Global Perspective*. Routledge.

Bruni, A. (2005). Shadowing Software and Clinical Records: On the Ethnography of Non-humans and Heterogeneous Contexts. *Organization, 12*(3), 357–378.

Bruni, A., Pinch, T., & Schubert, C. (2013). Technologically Dense Environments: What For? What Next? *Tecnoscienza, 4*(2), 51–72.

Cooren, F. (2020). Beyond Entanglement: (Socio-) Materiality and Organization Studies. *Organization Theory, 1*, 1–24.

Crouch, D. (2010). Flirting with Space: Thinking Landscape Relationally. *Cultural Geographies, 18*(1), 5–18.

Czarniawska, B. (2004). On Time, Space and Action Nets. *Organization, 11*(6), 777–795.

Gaver, W. W. (1991). Technology affordances. In *Proceedings of the SIGCHI conference on Human factors in computing systems Reaching through technology*.

Gibson, J. G. (1979). *The Ecological Approach to Visual Perception*. Houghton Mifflin.

Goffman, E. (1974). *Frame Analysis: An Essay on the Organization of Experience*. Harvard University Press.

Kiesling, S. F. (2013). Flirting and 'Normative' Sexualities. *Journal of Language and Sexuality, 2*(1), 101–121.

Kozin, A. (2016). Flirtation: Deconstructed. *Sexuality & Culture, 20,* 358–372.

Latour, B. (1992). *Aramis ou l'amour des techniques.* La Découverte.

Pinch, T. (2008). Technology and Institutions. *Theory and Society, 37,* 461–483.

Pinsky, D. (2019). Doing Gender Online Through Flirtation. *RESET, 8.*

Plesner, U., & Husted, E. (2019). *Digital Organizing.* Red Globe Press.

Polanyi, M. (1958). *Personal Knowledge. Towards a Post-Critical Philosophy.* Routledge.

Simmel, G. (1908). *Soziologie.* Dunker & Humblot.

Simmel, G. (1984 [1911]). *Georg Simmel: On Women, Sexuality, and Love* (pp. 133–152). Translated by OAKES Guy. New Haven: Yale University Press.

Speer, S. (2017). Flirting: A Designedly Ambiguous Action? *Research on Language and Social Interaction, 50*(2), 128–150.

Star, S.L. (1991), Invisible Work and Silenced Dialogues in Knowledge Representation, in I. Eriksson, B. Kitchenham, K. Tijdens, Women, Work and Computerization, , North Holland, pp. 81–92.

Star, S. L. (1999). The Ethnography of the Infrastructure. *American Behavioral Scientist, 43,* 377–391.

Steinhardt, S. B., & Jackson, S. J. (2015). Anticipation Work: Cultivating Vision in Collective Practice. In *Proc. CSCW 2015,* ACM Press.

Stone, A. S. (1995). *The War of Desire and Technology, at the Close of the Mechanical Age.* MIT Press.

Strati, A. (1999). *Organization and Aesthetics.* Sage.

Strauss, A., Fagerhaugh, S., Suczek, B., & Wiener, C. (1985). *The Social Organization of Medical Work.* University of Chicago Press.

Tavory, I. (2009). The Structure of Flirtation: On the Construction of Interactional Ambiguity. *Studies in Symbolic Interaction, 33,* 59–74.

Turnaturi, G. (1994). *Flirt, seduzione, amore. Simmel e le emozioni.* Anabasi.

Ullman, Y., Fodor, L., Schwarzberg, I., Carmi, N., Ullmann, A., & Yitzchak, R. (2008). The Sounds of Music in the Operating Room. *Injury, 39*(5), 592–597.

Whalen, J., Whalen, M., & Henderson, K. (2002). Improvisational Choreography in Teleservice Work. *British Journal of Sociology, 53*(2), 239–258.

CHAPTER 5

Communicating in the Operating Room: On the Mutual Relationship Between Technical Objects, Communicative Practices, and Organizing

Abstract This chapter delves into the role of objects and technologies in practices of organizational communication. It explores how communicative practices shape and are shaped by these elements in the operating room, and how objects and technologies actively participate in actions and conversations. Each activity in the operating room involves specific material devices and communicative acts, intertwining technology, communication, and organizational processes. The analysis focuses in particular on 'quick and fast' communicative practices, their mimetic nature, and the reciprocal relationship between objects and communication.

Finally, in relation to the communicative practices and the jargon that characterize everyday interactions in the operating room, also the gender dimension will emerge, giving the occasion to reflect on the gender(ed) dimension of sociomaterial practices.

Keywords Communicative practices • Mimetic communication • Technical objects • Gender practices

© The Author(s), under exclusive license to Springer Nature Switzerland AG 2023
A. Bruni, *Sociomaterial Practices in Medical Work*,
https://doi.org/10.1007/978-3-031-44804-1_5

5.1   On the Role of Communication in the Operating Room

To grasp the constitutive role communication practices have with respect to organizational processes and daily work in the operating room, it is sufficient to focus on a small interaction ritual, namely "calling the patient."

> The nurse anesthetist tells the room staff nurse that the operating room is ready and the patient can be transferred from the ward to the room. The room staff nurse thus reaches the phone in front of the sterilization room, phones the ward and asks to transport the patient to the room.

This fragment is telling of the importance of communication in the management of the surgery process: from an organizational point of view, it is a chain of face-to-face and remote communications between several operators (nurse anesthetist, room staff nurse, and ward staff) that activates the beginning of a surgical session. However, focusing on this small ritual already allows variations to be noted:

> The room staff nurse asks the surgeons: "May I call the other patient?". The surgeons, who are completing the surgery, answer affirmatively.
> There is still no one in the room, but after a while the first patient to be operated on arrives (transported by the room staff and nurse anesthetist).
> It is 8:00 a.m., but the patient has not yet arrived, so the nurse anesthetist asks the room staff nurse to fetch the patient from the ward and to have the next patient (the second on the list) ready as well, since the first surgery is expected to take a short time.

As from these excerpts, "calling the patient" is to some extent the result of shared work and widespread attention by different operators on the ongoing activities. From situation to situation, it is a different operator the one who "calls the patient," as in the case where it is the room staff nurse herself recalling the surgeons' attention to the opportunity of calling the next patient. Moreover, "calling the patient" is not sufficient in itself to ensure that the patient reaches the room in the expected time (in two cases, it is the anesthesia and the room staff nurse who activate to streamline the transport time), nor it is the case that the operating team is always present when the patient arrives. Finally, one does not necessarily have to wait until the end of surgery for "calling the patient"; indeed, this is often another of those anticipatory practices that allow actors to keep the rhythm of work. During the fieldwork, it was possible to witness how "calling the patient" in some cases represents a delicate passage point, as from the example to follow:

> The surgery (a breast implant) is about to be finished, the anesthesiologist asks whether to call the next patient, and the surgeon answers affirmatively. The anesthesiologist phones the department, but no one answers. At the same time, the surgeon realizes that he does not have the right size prosthesis and goes to the warehouse to look for it. The anesthesiologist tells him to tell the ward to prepare the next patient [but the surgeon will forget]. The operation stops for about 5 minutes, and when the surgeon returns, the anesthesiologist asks him how much time he needs to finish.
> Surgeon: "Half an hour!"
> Anesthesiologist: "But you answered me like that half an hour ago as well..."
> Surgeon: "Whatever...25 minutes."

As from this short excerpt, the practice of "calling the patient" may be subject to different modalities, also in relation to the additional elements of the activity at hand it associates with. Indeed, in the case just seen the fact that the prosthesis is not of the right size would not be a problem in itself, except that this dilutes the time of the surgery and that the next patient has already been called. Or rather, because of a series of miscommunications (the anesthesiologist phones the ward, but no one answers; the anesthesiologist tells the surgeon to report back to the ward to prepare the next patient, but the latter forgets), nobody 'calls' the patient (fortunately, since the surgeon needs another 30 minutes to finish the surgery).

The mismatch that sometimes arises between "calling the patient" and the moment when the latter is transported in the preoperative area and receives the attention of the operators depends on the unpredictability of the work in the operating room, but it also hooks into some communication practices. These include, first and foremost, the hasty and peremptory manner in which some surgeons sometimes reply to the solicitations of other operators. As from the final excerpt seen above, some surgeons in fact have an almost standard answer: "half an hour" (in case the surgery is still in progress) or "I'm done" (in case the surgery is over and the patient only needs to be sutured). However, the time the surgeon calculates does not take into account the timing of other operators: for example, the time it will take the anesthesiologist to awaken the patient, or the time it will take to the room staff nurse to clean the room and equip it for the next surgery (see Chap. 3).

All of these examples allow to frame "calling the patient" as a sociomaterial practice that involves the alignment of bodies, tools, spaces, times, and activities, and to grasp how communication is essential to achieving this alignment. This means that communication is not simply something that happens in organizations, but "the means by which organizations are established, composed, designed, and sustained" (Cooren et al., 2011: 1150). In this sense, a focus on a particular kind of communicative practice (so called "mimetic communication") will be of help in further illustrating the essential role communicative practices play in organizing.

5.2   MIMETIC COMMUNICATION: THE LANGUAGE OF EVERYDAY WORK

Workplace studies (Luff et al., 2000; Heath & Button, 2002) and ethnomethodological analysis of hospital work and communication (Pilnick et al., 2010) have variously showed how in healthcare settings, and particularly in anesthesia and surgery work, actors tend to manage space communicatively (Hindmarsh & Pilnick, 2002). For example, they create a backstage space by utilizing nonverbal communication outside of the patient's visual reach. Alternatively, it is possible that while speaking to the patient, the anesthesiologist directs messages to the nurse, thus conveying information and instructions that are concealed within ordinary conversation. Indeed, it should not be forgotten that in hospital settings 'communication' often means first and foremost making one's work manifest to other operators (Hindmarsh & Pilnick, 2002). The operating room is no exception, as from the following episodes:

> The anesthesiologist is trying to intubate the patient, but he cannot make it and has to resume manual ventilation. He tries a second time, but this also fails. At this point, he asks the room staff nurse who is in charge of transporting patients to ask in neurosurgery [the room next door] if they have a smaller laryngoscope. The room staff nurse returns saying no, so the nurse suggests the room staff nurse to try ask the cardiac surgery. The room staff nurse returns after a few minutes with the smaller laryngoscope, and the anesthesiologist manages to intubate the patient. After a moment, the Anesthesia Chief enters the room: "Everything okay?", he asks. The anesthesiologist replies: "Yes", and the Chief leaves the room. The anesthesiologist

comments: "It's a good thing there is this word of mouth... of course, he [the Chief of Anesthesia] could have arrived a little earlier..." [apparently, the 'voice' that the anesthesiologist was having problems intubating the patient immediately spread around the department].

The patient is transported to the operating room and placed on the bed. The anesthesiologist intubates him and then leaves the room, while the nurse anesthetist taps the peripheral vein. Dr. Gemma and Dr. Frigo enter the room, while the instruments nurse (Lia) inserts the bladder catheter to the patient. Meanwhile, Dr. Lago enters the room asking: "Ready?"; so he leaves the room without even waiting for an answer. A few minutes after the surgery begins: on the patient's right are Dr. Frigo and Lia, and on the left is Dr. Gemma. Dr. Lago enters the room and approaches the operating bed. The anesthesiologist goes into the hallway to ask the newly operated patient if he is in pain and then leaves. Meanwhile, the Chief enters the operating room and asks: "Have you started?"; then he goes to wash his hands. He comes back in a minute: now around the operating bed are three surgeons on the left and the Chief and Lia on the right. Lia says: "Someone to the light!", so the room staff nurse (Matteo) moves the operating light. Every time the Chief moves, the other three surgeons move in unison. Dr. Gemma says: "He's moving!", so the anesthesiologist gets up from the stool he was sitting on and administers a drug. Meanwhile, the Chief shouts: "The light is not necessary!" so Matteo arranges once again to move the operating light. The Chief moves and stands to the patient's left (the three surgeons make room for him and move to the other side of the operating bed), and Matteo follows him by moving the lamp. The Chief asks Lia for "big stitches", saying: "Give them to me! Give them to me, quick!" Matteo checks that the light is okay, counts the gauze, and checks that no needles fell into the bin of the dirty gauze.

In both excerpts, one can appreciate the operators' anticipatory work and the taking place of mostly silent and invisible coordination and communication processes. The first episode is meant to be illustrative of all those situations in which it is not necessary for an operator (an anesthesiologist, in our case) to explicitly ask for 'help' to have a more experienced colleague (the Chief, in our case) spontaneously supporting the ongoing process (not surprisingly, the anesthesiologist almost complains that word of mouth was not sufficiently rapid).

In the second episode, the verbal exchanges are kept to a minimum and are characterized by their speedy, fragmentary nature, and by serving mainly as a call for attention (addressed to those participating in the scene) and as a signal of what is about to be done. In this sense, "Ready?", "Have you started?", and "It's moving!" are expressions frequently used in the operating room and not addressed to any particular operator, but directed to recall the collective attention. But the episode is also representative of how working in advance constitutes one of the key skills not only of instruments nurses, but of all actors present in the operating room. As evidence of this, in the only two occasions when the Chief addresses other operators, the communication is directed at requesting more 'speed' in following processes and anticipating moves.

The main characteristic of what could be labeled as "mimetic communication" is then being directed at work activity, but at the same time not aimed at stimulating any kind of conversation and camouflaged within common sense expressions. From this point of view, the impression that a whole range of things in the operating room happen in an almost 'magical' way is the result of mimetic communication practices and of the invisible coordination work that, through such practices, actors enact.

The second excerpt also allows to note how communication not only takes place tacitly, but occurs through the body. Indeed, as within the choreography of a dance, it is important that the operators' movements around the operating table are coordinated and accompany each other, and that objects also follow and accompany these movements. As from the previous and next excerpt, the need for this constant alignment between bodies and technologies was clearly visible in relation to the use of the lamp, the positioning of which could easily be the cause of the surgeon's wrath:

> The surgeon (to the right of the patient) shouts at the room staff nurse: "How can you position the light the right way if you can't see what I see? You can't place the light the right way if you don't stand behind me!". So the room staff nurse (who had been standing to the patient's left until now) positions himself behind the surgeon.

Conversely, it was this following the other's body that allowed the operators to better manage the alignment between bodies and technologies:

> The first surgeon lets the second surgeon finishing the patient's suture and steps away from the operating bed. While the second surgeon is suturing, the room staff nurse says to him: "What if I lift the bed for you? Because some positions are a bit dangerous..." [the operator refers to the fact that

the surgeon is forced to work bent almost at a ninety-degree angle because of the height of the bed, which is calibrated to the body of the former surgeon]. The patient is anesthetized and strapped to the bed, in that she has to be placed in a sitting position for the surgery. As the bed rises, the instruments nurse says: "It's coming down...", and the surgeon replies: "Of course it's coming down, it has to come down...." The instruments nurse replies, "Yes, I was looking at the tube..." [which is not of the right length and might come off].

As already noted in reference to other episodes (see Chap. 3), there is a complex interplay of movements and material reminders that takes shape between humans and technological objects. Differently from other episodes, however, these excerpts highlight the importance played by language and communication in giving visibility to these mutual positionings, and maintaining a good level of coordination within the team. Communication is essential to draw actors' attention to the alignments necessary to perform the work correctly and to make visible the possible entanglements of bodies and technologies (as in the case where the instruments draw the surgeon's attention to the length of a tube to which the patient's body is connected).

Although largely mimetic, communicative practices keep trace of the sociomaterial dimension of medical work, while contributing to its expression. In order to illustrate this dynamic in more details, we will now consider first how objects and technologies participate in processes and practices of organizational communication; later on, we will turn to the illustration of how communicative practices perform objects and technologies.

5.3   Objects and Technologies in Practices of Organizational Communication

Objects and technologies are constantly present in the words of surgeons, anesthesiologists, and nurses. This is partly due to the fact that in organizations a considerable portion of communications have an institutional character. Institutional conversation (Drew & Heritage, 1992) is directly stimulated by the organizational context, explicitly oriented to the accomplishment of work, and usually dependent on the technical universe (machines, objects, tools) and the professional vocabulary typical of the context of reference. In the operating room, one of the most explicit examples of such communications is offered by the so-called "swap" of operators (i.e., when the handover between operators takes place), as from the following examples:

> The room staff nurse passes some information to the colleague who is swapping with him, namely the number of gauzes used, the number of laparotomies, and the time when the carotid "plaque" was sent to the laboratory.
> The nurse anesthetist informs her colleague, who is ready to take over, that 45 cl out of the 110 cl of blood entered into the machine has been reinjected into the patient and gives indications about the drugs administered and those to be administered. Meanwhile, the room staff nurse who has finished her work shift informs the colleague who will relieve her of the number of gauze pads already counted.

Being *per se* moments in which the communication is explicitly directed toward the accomplishment of work, when "swapping" the vocabulary of operators becomes mainly technical and an entire material world made of drugs, technical and medical devices, bodies, organs, and prosthesis emerges. But objects and technologies are omnipresent in actors' words also because frequently they become matter of discussion, as from these short excerpts:

> The instruments nurse is not quick enough in passing the irons to the surgeon [meaning that she does not have ready in their hands the irons the surgeon will need to continue the surgery], so that the surgeon says (raises the tone of his voice): "I mean…do you know what irons are to be used or not?!"
> The patient is asleep and after intubation Sabrina inserts the bladder catheter. Meanwhile, Dr. Zeta enters the room and says: "Not ready yet? Come on, Sabrina!"
> Sabrina replies: "I'll be ready…when I'll be ready!"
> Dr. Zeta: "Of course…it takes you half an hour just to insert the catheter!"
> Dr. Zappalà enters the operating room and seeing that Sonia (the instruments nurse) is still preparing the irons for the next surgery, he says: "Sonia, we are ready…". Sonia answers: "I'm ready as well, just give me the time to finishing preparing [the irons needed for the next surgery]."

During the fieldwork, it was more than common to observe actors quarreling (sometimes in a highly vivid way) around objects and technical devices: the operating block head-charge nurse frequently discusses with surgeons and anesthesiologists regarding the proper use of personal protection equipment; surgeons comply if nurses do not handle irons fast enough and the latter get nervous when surgeons put pressure on them because of irons; room staff nurses are constantly asked about gauzes and other technical equipment and immediately reproved in case they do not know what to answer; anesthesiologists complain about the space they have in the operating room for their technical equipment. The list could continue, but the point is that differently from institutional conversation, in all these cases various objects and technologies enter the conversation as 'objective' demonstrations of actors' skills. In particular, the main skill refers to how fast operators are in managing technical devices, so that through language irons and catheters become sorts of labor (and actors) speed detectors.

From a sociomaterial point of view, thus, we witness how communication is not only grounded in the technical universe of everyday work, but how objects and technologies act at various levels in processes and practices of organizational communication. They may perform routines, controversies, stress, nervousness, or expertise, increasing the degrees of materiality words and discourse have.

5.4 Performing Objects and Technologies Through Communicative Practices

In order for a technology to properly function, users always have to perform some kind of more or less visible work. Sometimes, this less visible work regards the ways in which actors accompany the use of a technology with words or sentences aimed at anticipating some of its features, as from the following excerpts:

> Giada (nurse anesthetist) reaches the pre-room and helps the patient to the operating bed. The room assistant nurse straps the patient's arm to the armrest of the bed while Giada says: "Now I'm going to attach some wires to you."
> The surgery requires local anesthesia and the patient is already on the operating table when the surgeon (Dr. Bianco) approaches the operating table and says: "Now you will feel two pokes for local anesthesia."

In these two cases, actors communicate to patients the appearance of a technical instrument differently. In the first case, the technical device is presented in quite neutral terms ("Now I'm going to attach some wires to you"), while in the second, it is associated to something painful ("Now you will feel two pokes for local anesthesia"). In both cases, by the way, by anticipating discursively the presence and the effects of a technology, operators support its acceptance, use, and performance: wires and needles are different and may have different effects on patients, but talking about them acts as a form of justification and naturalization of their presence and effects. From this point of view, it can be viewed as part of the sentimental work (Strauss et al., 1985) nurses perform when administering drugs or therapeutic treatments.

In other occasions, the relevance of verbal communications in supporting technology's use and performance was particularly explicit, as from the next excerpts:

> The anesthesiologist tells the patient that the surgery will take place in local anesthesia, so that she will remain awake and at any time she should feel "tremors in her legs or arms" or "strange", she should have told it right away.
>
> During the surgery (under spinal anesthesia), the nurse anesthetist continually checks the monitor and talks to the patient, asking her if she is okay, if she is comfortable, and telling her that the surgery is about to be completed.

The two excerpts are representative of the many different situations in which communication is essential in order to monitor technology and to check what technology itself cannot check: that is, how and/or what the patient feels. In the first excerpt, communicating with the patient is crucial in order to involve him/her as an active detector and communicative agent of possible anesthesia side effects. The second excerpt shows a somehow complementary dynamic, in which the operator continuously talks to the patient, asking questions about her comfort and her feeling "ok" that the monitor could never answer. In both cases, thus, communications between operators and patients emerge as a crucial way not only for supporting and integrating the information given by technology, but to perform technology itself. Through communications, actors give voice to what technologies should or should not do, thus materializing parts of their processes and effects.

Pairing the action of technologies with words, actors keep machines and bodies aligned, adding coherence to the performance of technologies. Through words, actors may indeed vanish technological action, as shown by the next ethnographic excerpt:

> During a surgery, dr. Zeta asks the nurse anesthetist to check the ultrasound and read the endocrinologist's report. The nurse reads it and Zeta listens in silence, merely nodding. Then, he asks the nurse to read the ultrasound and the result again, to find out if "there are nodules on the right." The nurse reads the result again and says there are no nodules on the right, only on the left.
>
> Later on, the phone rings: apparently the ones removed are not the "right" nodules. So, Zeta resumes the surgery and looks for other nodules: this time he finds them, but on the right, not the left. "But if they can't even distinguish right from left. Either they misread the ultrasound or it was a slip...I hope." Apparently, the doctor who wrote the report mentioned the presence of nodules on the left, but they were on the right.

In this episode, the surgeon relies on the nurse anesthetist to read the ultrasound report and confirm the presence of nodules on the right side. However, the ultrasound report 'says' that there are no nodules on the right side, only on the left. It is thanks to a different technology (the telephone) and other actors (the operators who checked if the nodules were the right ones) that the surgeon is informed that there should be other nodules. While ultrasound technology can provide visual evidence of the presence and location of nodules, the surgeon had to rely on verbal communication to confirm his suspicions. It is worth noticing that the misreporting provided by the endocrinologist regarding the location of the nodules cancels the opportunity offered by the technology to visualize the nodules and the work done by the ultrasound. Thus, an initial 'slip' in the report of the examination causes a breakdown in the overall communication process between the medical professionals involved in the surgery and in the surgical process itself, highlighting the relevance of human communication (in written and spoken forms) for the effective integration of technological tools in healthcare settings.

5.5   COMMUNICATIVE PRACTICES: WHEN GENDER MATTERS

Communicative practices in the operating room are not simply marked by technical objects and do not just perform objects and technologies. They are also marked by and oriented toward the reproduction of a masculinity constructed along the lines of heroism and bravado (Bruni, 2012), and which finds expression in women's subordination toward men and in a hegemonic model of cathexis (Connell, 1995). As narrated by a female surgeon: "*My Chief surgeon used to tell me: 'If you're afraid of getting stung, change profession… go work as a secretary!'*" The account is undoubtedly partial, but prescient of what we shall see to be the lines of expression of gender stereotypy in the observed organizational environment and of the ancillary role attributed to women and the feminine. Moreover, it clearly positions women as belonging to an 'other' professional self: evoking the figure of a 'secretary,' the Chief surgeon makes explicit how women in the professional community of surgeons are not generic newcomers. They belong to a gendered category, that of women, and enter an organizational and professional *milieu* dominated by values, symbols, and artifacts whose maleness is taken for granted and which yields a 'position rent' and a competitive advantage to men and masculinity (Bruni & Gherardi, 2001). Indeed, the Chief surgeon himself used to enter the operating room not wearing cap and mask, and (sometimes) in an undershirt, thus reiterating how the use of personal protective equipment and adherence to rules are intertwined with professional status and the associated displays of virile masculinity. How likely would it be for a female surgeon to enter the operating room in an undershirt?

Another channel for the expression and manifestation of bravado was then provided by the 'jokes,' the 'teasing,' and the 'attentions' male surgeons and anesthesiologists directed at female staff (usually, instrument nurses and nurses), as in the case to follow:

"Where is the instrumentalist? You have to stay behind me!", the surgeon says. He needs the lamp to be moved, so the instrument nurse (Marta) gets on the platform placed behind the surgeon and moves the lamp. "Well done, Marta! How would I do without you!", says the surgeon as he proceeds with the removal of a trachea.

The surgeon notices my presence[1] and asks me who I am, who commissioned the research, and where do I come from. I answer his questions and explain the object of the research. He continues: "What did you find? Did you write that we are sex maniacs? But it's all Marta's fault, you know?!" [Marta and the two newcomer surgeons smile fictitiously].

The surgeon invites me to take a closer look at the surgery and says: "We are holding a trachea. However, believe me, you should do some studies on sex maniacs to understand more about us... Don't write! Don't write!"

Marta meanwhile gets off the platform and goes to get the container inside which to insert a removed lymph node, but immediately the surgeon calls her back: "Marta! The light! Where did it go?" Marta places the container on the table, climbs onto the platform and moves the light. The surgeon: "Are you potty training? I'd be curious to see you ...."[2]

After a long series of sexual innuendos, the surgeon narrates how he "tested" a newcomer instrument nurse by: "doing psychological terrorism, telling her take this, give me that ...".

The reported episode is sadly representative of all the recurrent situations in which male surgeons and anesthesiologists acted out their interaction with female instrument nurses and nurse anesthetists on the axes of the stereotyped sexual relations that should/could occur between men and women. It is what Timmons and Tanner (2005) have named in terms of the "hostess role," emphasizing how much of nursing work in the operating room revolves around "making the surgeon happy" and/or "not irritating the surgeon." After all, this harks back to the very characteristics that from a historical perspective have marked the nursing profession: as a caring professional, the nurse easily appears as a professional translation of the domestic role of women in European societies, with all its characteristics of devotion, passivity, and sacrifice (Holden & Littlewood, 1991).

As well known in the literature on gender and organization (Calàs & Smircich, 1992; Gherardi, 1996), this is a strategy that aims at reducing to a biological dimension women's skills that are considered "naturally" feminine (such as listening, managing conflicts, or caring), while at the same

---

[1] The researcher here is a woman.

[2] The expression "potty training" is used in Italian as a colloquial (and unpolite) way of referring to the act of urinating or defecating in the potty or toilet. It is a commonly used expression when referring to the process of training children in the use of the potty or toilet during the transition from diaper to toilet use, but it is also a figurative and unpolite way of referring to somebody who is too slow or not competent enough in the performance of an activity.

time denigrating identities not aligned with the dominant form of masculinity (Bruni, 2006). Moreover, it should be noted how the surgeon deploys toward the female researcher the same relational game enacted with the instrument nurse, trying to embarrass her by directing the discourse on sex, while impressing her by showing a trachea, and giving her orders and demonstrations of his power toward other operators. In this sense, even the way in which surgeons and anesthesiologists related to my colleague and me is probably symptomatic of the gendered citizenship (Gherardi, 1996) reserved for men and women in this organizational environment: the female researcher was on several occasions the object of jokes, appreciations, and puns based on sex and gender; being a male researcher, on the other hand, I found myself involved in language games with an equally obvious sexual background, but these more often took the form of a search for male complicity, rather than defiance or awe.

But sex-oriented language games were only the most obvious translation of doing gender (West & Zimmerman, 1987) within the operating room and in the course of work practices. In somewhat more general terms, it can be said that there is an entire nexus of practices (Hui et al., 2016) moving along the lines of gender in the operating room. Different types of positioning (Davies & Harré, 1990) are possible, and now we will see some of the main tactics (De Certeau, 1980) women share to position themselves as competent participants within a community whose gender order relegates them to a role of subalternity.

5.6   Gender as Sociomaterial Practice

Through what practices and positionings do women manage to break out of the "hostess role" so easily and frequently assigned to them?

A first practice and positioning have to do with silence, as in the following episode:

> When the first surgeon enters the room, he immediately addresses the operating surgeon: "But… are you alone today, doctor?"
> D.: "There's him…" [a newcomer surgeon]
> S.: "Whatever… what about Franchi?" [the other surgeon expected today]
> D.: "He just phoned me… he has a cold, but he said he's on his way…"
> And so, a whole series of jokes between the surgeon and other practitioners about the causes of Dr. Franchi's cold begin. "Women he fucks with leave him uncovered overnight…" says the surgeon, trying to involve the

anesthesiologist and nurse anesthetist in the conversation, but the latter do not participate.

Situations and 'jokes' such as the one just described were the norm in the operating room as in other spaces of the operating block, to the point that one operator during the first days of observation (after looking at the composition of the operating team and referring to a surgeon in particular) explicitly warned the researcher: "*There will be constant sex jokes. It's a bit like that in all the rooms, but here especially... when he* [the starring surgeon of the previous episode] *is present.*"

In these situations, nonparticipating to the conversation (as the female nurse anesthetist does) is not a symptom of embarrassment or passivity, but it constitutes a practice of resistance to the camaraderie climate that men try to establish by mobilizing (Martin, 2001) various practices of masculinity. In this particular case, these refer to a male-oriented heterosexual humor, but the same kind of attitude was also adopted by female nurses in situations in which male surgeons and anesthesiologists used vulgar or aggressive language, shouted, and/or directed gratuitous and stigmatizing criticism and epithets toward other colleagues or operators. The nonparticipation, the silent acting of female instrument nurses and nurse anesthetists carves out a different space and practice within which surgeon cannot enter precisely because embracing such a practice would mean having to abandon a swaggering attitude.

It could be argued that silence in symbolic terms refers to the feminine anyhow, and thus interpret this practice as a way of positioning within the boundaries of the sex/gender system (Rubin, 1975), rather than as the construction of an autonomous space from the masculine. However, one should keep in mind that confronting surgeons directly within a professional and organizational culture marked by such an entrenched gender repertoire and a highly structured distribution of power was taken by most surgeons as a real affront. Given that bravado and susceptibility share the same semantic field, arguing with surgeons could easily lead to situations like the one to follow:

[the researcher enters the room]
    The surgeon shouts to the anesthesiologist: "Doctor, the patient is moving!". The anesthesiologist gets up from the stool she was sitting on, takes a syringe and administers a drug to the patient. Then she adds: "Anyway, you cannot answer "I don't give a shit" to me!"

Surgeon: "Are you kidding!!!?"

Anesthesiologist: "No. You just answered me that way".

The surgeon for a moment stands still and stops operating, but noticing the anesthesiologist moving away from the room, starts shouting: "The patient's bleeding! The patient's bleeding! Anesthesiologist! Where is the anesthesiologist? I don't see her!"

The anesthesiologist, in front of the door of the room, replies: "Here I am!"

Surgeon: "You must stay here, behind the patient! And don't answer me! Now you won't even be able to go pee without my permission!"

The anesthesiologist says nothing, no one says anything. Complete silence has fallen in the room. The surgery is now at a critical point: the surgeon inserts a pouch into one of the three holes drilled in the abdomen, transfers (with the help of some needles) the excised tumor into the pouch, closes it (with some 'grafettes') and then (with forceps) pulls one end out of the hole from which he had inserted it. Then, with his hands, he pulls the bag. However, the part removed is larger in diameter than the hole he drilled, so the surgeon has to pull hard to succeed in pulling it out. When, after a few attempts, he succeeds, the surgeon pricks himself with one of the 'grafettes'.

Surgeon: "God damn!"

Instrument nurse: "Take off your gloves!"

Surgeon removes gloves and puts on a clean pair, then goes on: "He's moving! Shall we do something?"

The anesthesiologist, without saying anything, administers more drugs. After the discussion between the two, the nurse anesthetist did not leave the room either, but sat by the ventilator in silence the whole time.

Surgeon: "Now let's put on an emergency! Is that okay with you doctor?!?"

It is 1:20 p.m. and the surgery has yet to be completed. Usually, at this time operating sessions stop, but the surgeon insists. At 1:40 p.m. the surgeon "closes" the operating field and leaves the operating room without saying anything.

The researcher was not present in the room at the time the anesthesiologist claims the surgeon uttered the fateful phrase, so it is not known what exactly happened in the moments before the reported interaction. However, as famously noted by Strauss (quoted in Star, 1991), from an interactionist point of view, the consequences of social action are important as its causes. Regardless of the underlying cause, the situation is indicative of the stressful atmosphere that sometimes prevails in the operating room where most of the observations took place; of how the bravado which seems to mark surgeons' professional attitude can result in unsafe practices toward patients and operators themselves; of how conflicts between operators are managed mainly through practices inscribed in the symbolic realm of masculinity, and which refer to the exercise of authority, hierarchy, threat, and control over other actors' body ("*Now you won't even be able to go pee without my permission!*" is one of the first threats the surgeon addresses to the anesthesiologist).

As in the situation seen earlier, the instrument nurse remains silent (and helps the surgeon changing gloves), but it would be hasty to conclude that the only two possible positionings for women within this environment move between the two extremes of silent action and direct confrontation.

In this regard, two ethnographic excerpts are particularly representative of both the practices of masculinity that characterize the operating block and the symbolic positionings that women can enact. As a deliberate choice, reference will be made to situations that take place outside the operating room, in order to show how a gendered (masculine) repertoire is at work in the most common communicative practices that characterize the observed environment, constituting therefore a background element of different interactions.

> A pharmaceutical sales representative is chatting with the Head instrument nurse. They talk about this and that, but when the discourse comes to a female doctor who is objecting to no-latex gloves, the salesman says the doctor's grievances are dictated purely by stress and dissatisfaction: "It would take a nigger, to give her two strokes....". The Head nurse replies: "And why don't you take care of it?!?"
>
> Dr. Zeta is chatting with the Head Nurse of the Surgery ward. They enter the nurses' office, where a doctor is filling out a medical record, one nurse is making a photocopy, another is rinsing containers and two more nurses are filling some documents. The Head Nurse exclaims: "Here they are, the showgirls!". Zeta takes the opportunity to immediately add some sexist jokes, and only one nurse shyly protests. The Head Nurse adds: "In my view, you [nurses] are too many... first thing to do [following the appointment of the new Chief Nurse]: reduce the staff!"

The two presented situations are distinct from each other: in the first one, two individuals are involved, while in the second one, a group is involved. In the first situation, the Head Nurse attempts to expose through irony the gender and racial stereotypes employed by the salesman, whereas in the second one, it is the Head nurse herself who triggers them. However, in processual terms, the two situations also exhibit certain similarities: in both instances, gender and sex emerge as the most immediate, obvious, and thus 'natural' references in order to make sense of the situation; in both cases, women are defined as objects of an assumed and unspecified male heterosexual desire; in both cases, gender stereotypes manifest through communicative performances that strive to appear 'humorous,' but which instead appear irredeemably gratuitous, vulgar, and discriminatory.

For the purpose of the present discussion, what is of particular interest is the discursive positioning enacted by the two Head nurses. In the first situation, we witness an ironic positioning, through which the Head instrument nurse demonstrates her competence in managing a discursive repertoire oriented toward the masculine and, simultaneously, in destabilizing its order. It is noteworthy how irony resides not merely in the content of the remark articulated by the Head nurse, but primarily in the fact that it is she, a woman, who utters such a phrase, challenging her interlocutor on his own symbolic terrain. The exercise of irony, moreover, represents one of the most common practices of transgressing gender symbolic boundaries within organizational contexts, particularly by individuals belonging to stigmatized categories such as women (Gherardi, 1995).

In the second episode as well, the Head nurse employs a playful tone and demonstrates her competence in conforming to a masculine communicative code, but differently from her colleague not to transgress gender norms. Instead, she pays homage to the masculine by discursively repositioning the female nurses in their role of women in service of men and flattening their competencies to mere support for male agency (*"Here they are... the showgirls!"*). As in the previous case, it is not only language but the entire situation that is performative in itself in terms of gender boundaries crossing: labeling female nurses as "showgirls" allows the Head nurse (a woman) to distinguish herself from them and discursively mobilize a particularly masculine version of power and human resource management (*"there are too many of you... first thing to do: reduce the staff!"*).

In both situations, therefore, we witness a crossing of conventional gender boundaries through the mobilization of a masculine discursive repertoire, but for different purposes. This raises an age-old question: when a woman enters a professional and/or organizational culture marked by practices of masculinity, can she handle these practices so skillfully as to subvert a masculine subject position (Kerfoot & Whitehead, 1998; Bruni & Gherardi, 2001; Gherardi & Poggio, 2007)? Or within a context of hegemonic masculinity (Carrigan et al., 1985; Connell, 1995), by definition women cannot enjoy the privileges of the masculine and can at best position themselves in opposition to "emphasized femininity" (i.e., all those behaviors and symbols typical of femininity aimed at confirming and satisfying masculine stereotypes and desires—Connell, 1995)?

These questions have long plagued the debate and highlight a common 'formal flaw' in contemporary gender studies investigating empirically how men perform masculinity and women perform femininity. These studies reinforce an assumed correspondence between sex and gender, within a theoretical perspective that posits the nonautomatic alignment between biological sex and gender practices.

As a partial remedy to this *impasse*, I propose an extensive use of the concept of mobilizing masculinities as defined by Patricia Martin (2001), which refers to all practices through which two or more men collaboratively invoke (discursively and interactively) elements related to the exercise of different forms of masculinity. By "extensive use," I refer to the fact that the concept can also be applied to situations (such as the ones analyzed) where women, in collaboration with other participants in the interaction context, bring into play elements that evoke masculine practices and/or worlds. Analytically, this allows to shift the focus definitively from the individual subject (and her/his sexual identity) performing the "mobilization" to the types of practices being mobilized and the forms of mobilization. This is not to assert the irrelevance of individual's identity characteristics, but rather to concentrate on how practices themselves (and not just the individuals) cross the boundaries of masculinity and femininity.

Indeed, one should bear in mind that the construction of a bravado professional imaginary finds fertile ground in other characteristics that the work in the operating room (and, more generally, in hospital settings) expresses in terms of gender (Bruni, 2012):

- the heroic dimension with which surgeons often speak of (and act out) the daily work;
- the cold and detached attitude that many anesthesiologists display in the course of operations;
- the ancillary position that characterizes some professional figures (typically, the room staff nurse, the anesthesiologist nurse, and the instrument nurse);

- the care, attention, and silent action that characterize the work of instrument nurses;
- the position of explicit subordination that marks the initial stages of the surgeons' learning trajectory;
- the removal of the patient (and of her or his body) as a living subject, so to turn it into an inert object.

In the operating room, all these elements inscribe work in a gender imaginary much more devoted to the masculine than to the feminine, likely fueled by the presumed superiority and authority attributed to medical knowledge and the medical profession in western cultures (Holden & Littlewood, 1991).

REFERENCES

Bruni, A. (2006). 'Have You Got a Boyfriend or are You Single?': On the Importance of Being 'Straight' in Organizational Research. *Gender, Work and Organization, 3*(3), 299–316.

Bruni, A. (2012). Attraverso la maschilità: posizionamenti e sconfinamenti di genere in sala operatoria. *AboutGender, 1*(2). Retrieved from https://riviste.unige.it/aboutgender/article/view/33

Bruni, A., & Gherardi, S. (2001). Omega's Story: The Heterogeneous Engineering of a Gendered Professional Self. In M. Dent & S. Whitehead (Eds.), *Managing Professional Identities. Knowledge, Performativity and the New Professional* (pp. 174–198). Routledge.

Calàs, M., & Smircich, L. (1992). Re-writing Gender into Organizational Theorizing: Directions from Feminist Perspectives. In M. I. Reed & M. D. Hughes (Eds.), *Rethinking Organizations: New Directions on Organizational Research and Analysis.* Sage.

Carrigan, T., Connell, R. W., & Lee, J. (1985). Toward a New Sociology of Masculinity. *Theory and Society, 14*(5), 551–603.

Connell, R. W. (1995). *Masculinities.* University of California Press.

Cooren, F., Kuhn, T., Cornelissen, J. P., & Clark, T. (2011). Communication, Organizing and Organization: An Overview and Introduction to the Special Issue. *Organization Studies, 32*(9), 1149–1170.

Davies, B., & Harré, R. (1990). Positioning: The Discursive Production of Selves. *Journal of the Theory of Social Behaviour, 20*(1), 43–63.

de Certeau, M. (1980). *L'invention du quotidien. Vol. 1, Arts de faire.* Paris: Union générale d'éditions; Engl. Transl., *The Practice of Everyday Life.* Berkeley: University of California Press, 1984.

Drew, P., & Heritage, J. (1992). Analyzing Talk at Work: An Introduction. In P. Drew & J. Heritage (Eds.), *Talk at Work* (pp. 3–65). Cambridge University Press.

Gherardi, S. (1995). *Gender, Symbolism and Organizational Cultures.* Sage.

Gherardi, S. (1996). Gendered Organizational Cultures: Narratives of Women Travellers in a Male World. *Gender, Work and Organization, 3*(4), 187–201.

Gherardi, S., & Poggio, B. (2007). *Gendertelling in Organizations: Narratives from Male-dominated Environments.* Liber.

Heath, C., & Button, G. (2002). Special Issue on Workplace Studies: Editorial Introduction. *The British Journal of Sociology, 53*(2), 157–161.

Hindmarsh, J., & Pilnick, A. (2002). The Tacit Order of Teamwork: Collaboration and Embodied Conduct in Anesthesia. *The Sociological Quarterly, 43,* 139–164.

Holden, P., & Littlewood, E. (Eds.). (1991). *Anthropology and Nursing.* Routledge.

Hui, S., Shove, E., & Schatzki, T. (Eds.). (2016). *The Nexus of Practices: Connections, Constellations, and Practitioners.* Routledge.

Kerfoot, D., & Whitehead, S. (1998). Boys Own' Stuff: Masculinity and the Management of Further Education. *The Sociological Review, 46*(3), 437–457.

Luff, P., Hindmarsh, J., & Heath, C. (2000). *Workplace Studies. Recovering Work Practice and Informing System Design.* Cambridge University Press.

Martin, P. Y. (2001). 'Mobilizing Masculinities'. Women's Experience of Men at Work. *Organization, 8*(4), 587–618.

Pilnick, A., Hindmarsh, J., & Jill, V. T. (2010). *Communication in Healthcare Settings: Policy, Participation and New Technologies.* Wiley-Blackwell.

Rubin, G. (1975). The Traffic in Women: Notes on the 'Political Economy' of Sex. In R. Reiter (Ed.), *Towards an Anthropology of Women* (pp. 23–65). Monthly Review Press.

Star, S. L. (1991). The Sociology of the Invisible: The Primacy of Work in the Writings of Anselm Strauss. In D. R. Maines (Ed.), *Social Organization and Social Process* (pp. 265–283). De Gruyter.

Strauss, A., Fagerhaugh, S., Suczek, B., & Wiener, C. (1985). *The Social Organization of Medical Work.* University of Chicago Press.

Timmons, S., & Tanner, J. (2005). Operating Theatre Nurses: Emotional Labour and the Hostess Role. *International Journal of Nursing Practice, 11*(2), 85–91.

West, C., & Zimmerman, D. (1987). Doing Gender. *Gender & Society, 1*(2), 125–151.

CHAPTER 6

Learning the Trade: Professional Visions and Organizational Power at Work

Abstract This chapter examines the diverse professional expertise and knowledge present in the operating room. It explores how actors hold distinct professional visions and logics, which can lead to disagreements in actions, patient positioning, and room setup. Fieldnotes' interpretation reveals the various professional visions that shape the evaluations and decisions of organizational actors. Additionally, it emphasizes the role of objects and technologies in constructing and performing professional knowledge. In particular, the chapter highlights the symbiotic materialism and material awareness a professional vision implies, together with the sensemaking processes it is intertwined with. Finally, the discussion concentrates on how power materializes in the relationships between different professionals, giving rise to peculiar sociomaterial choreographies.

Keywords Professional vision • Symbiotic materialism • Material awareness • Power dynamics

6.1 Professional Vision and Symbiotic Materialism

The different professional logics and visions present in the operating room usually take shape with reference to three situations: (1) in planning the timing of the surgery; (2) with reference to the positioning of the patient

A. Bruni, *Sociomaterial Practices in Medical Work*, https://doi.org/10.1007/978-3-031-44804-1_6

on the operating table; (3) when there are operators who are not used to work together.

Of the first situation, we have already seen several testimonies both in the section about technologies (see Chap. 3) and in the one about communication (see Chap. 4): being focused on 'the surgery,' surgeons often do not take into account the time needed for preparing the operating room, washing the irons, and setting up the surgical instruments. In the same way, the time needed in the ward for the preparation of the next patient is not always taken into account in the operating room, which can lead to the paradoxical (but frequent) situation where everything and everyone is ready except for the patient, who is absent because not "ready" yet.

The background of these misalignments in timing and of the resulting interactions is given by the different professional logics and visions that actors develop in the course of their daily work. The concept of 'professional vision' (Goodwin, 1994—see Chap. 1) frames professional competence as the result of knowledge that rests on a set of theoretical notions, but which is refined in the course of daily work experience and in relation to specific tools and materials, until it becomes embodied (hence, the famous 'clinical eye' in medicine).

Thus, it is the refinement of a particular professional vision that allows (for example) instrument nurses to pass instruments to/surgeons without the latter having to ask for them; surgeons to immediately recognize the quality of a suture; anesthesiologists to intubate patients without encountering difficulties; and room staff nurse to move within the operating room without hindering the movements of other operators. From this point of view, the time reserved for the novices' training period seems more than justified: in the case of instrument nurses, this can take up to a year, and the same is true for anesthesiologists and nurse anesthetists. Different, in a sense, is the case of surgeons, who start operating during their postgraduate residency, but on the other hand follow a particularly protracted learning trajectory, spending years assisting more experienced colleagues.

The development of a professional vision is thus closely related to the environment in which the activity takes place and to the more experienced figures one meets and with whom s/he has the opportunity to collaborate, as in the case to follow:

The anesthesiologist intubates the patient, so the surgery can begin. The two surgeons disinfect the surgical field and place sterile drapes over the woman's body. The room staff nurse, soon after, at the surgeon's direction, changes the bed position, placing the patient in a sitting position. At this point, the nurse anesthetist tells her novice colleague: "Always watch out when patients are moved, because some wires or the IV may come off."

In the excerpt just seen, an experienced nurse calls the attention of a newcomer colleague to a detail evidently derived from experience (paying attention to the wires when changing the positioning of the patient). The communication is concise (as already noted in the previous chapter, verbal exchanges in the operating room are kept to a minimum), but probably effective, as it is explicitly addressed to the colleague and with a prescriptive incipit (*"Always watch out"*). The communication is intended to recall the attention of the novice not to the patient him/herself, but to the materials (wires, IV) attached to him or her, and which (differently from his/her body) should not move.

The excerpt is thus meant to be representative of both the relevance of interacting with more experienced colleagues in order to acquire a professional vision, and the difficulty of separating the making of that vision from the specific material setting that shape the activity. More than a symbiotic gesture (Goodwin, 2003—see Chap. 1), what we witness here is a kind of 'symbiotic materialism': the entire material setting is an integral component of the activity itself. Indeed, what is sometimes surprising about the daily work in the operating room is the competence that all experienced operators demonstrate in articulating a variety of materials and, in turn, in following (often invisibly) each other's activity. Consider the following episodes:

The instrument nurse, noticing that the room staff nurse is busy counting gauze, asks the nurse anesthetist to bring her some water from the sterilization room.

The more experienced surgeon leaves the operating room telling his younger colleague to finish "closing" the patient. The instrument nurse positions herself in front of the surgeon (where the other surgeon was standing before) and passes him the irons, while also operating with the electric scalpel at the surgeon's request.

While waiting for the instrument nurse to finish preparing the irons for a new surgery, Mario (nurse anesthetist) prepares the patient in the pre-room, getting help from Francesca (a novice nurse anesthetist). After a couple of minutes, Mario notices that the instrument nurse has finished and that everything is ready in the operating room, but Dr. Ponte (the anesthesiologist) has left the room. Mario tells Francesca: "You get him [the patient] ready, I'll see if I can find Dr. Ponte," and he leaves the room.

In the proposed excerpts, we can see how as much as the tasks of the members of the surgical team are defined, there is a constant rearrangement of roles and activities, based on contingent events and needs. The main competence of the operators (regardless of their professional affiliation) lies precisely in this ability of continuously rearticulating tasks among the participants in the operating session, which often means to look after the different materials medical practices involve. In all the episodes just seen, actors pay attention to each other's action and simultaneously to the technical objects involved by that action (irons, electric scalpel, gauze, water). Actors constantly monitor the situation by considering its material components, as when the nurse anesthetist decides to leave the room and look after the anesthesiologist given that the irons for the new surgery are ready.

In the case of some professional figures, this ability is appropriately stimulated during the training period. The learning path of instrumental nurses, for example, requires them also to perform room service, since (as expressed by a newly appointed instrument nurse): "*Doing room service is useful anyway, because you learn where the irons are, what they are called. We come out of school without ever having seen an iron. Here's where we learn everything.*" It is then this widespread knowledge of the technical objects involved by work practices that allow the instrument nurses not only to work in advance, but also to undertake and othertake (Latour, 2005) action in all those situations in which other operators are absent.

6.2   Professional Vision Meets Patients' Body

Professional visions are entangled with technical objects also in reference to the positioning of the patients. In most cases, different professional skills and visions are mutually supportive and accompanying, as from the following episodes:

The instrument nurse asks if the next patient (a mastectomy) should be positioned sitting up, and the surgeon answers affirmatively. The anesthesiologist enters the room and says: "We're going to have her sit up awake so we can see how she slides, and then, if it's okay, we'll have her lie down." Everyone agrees.

The team discusses positioning the patient: the instrument nurse suggests putting a pillow under her shoulders, but the surgeon disagrees because she would not be able to stretch her neck. After a few minutes, a compromise is reached: the headboard is lowered.

One of the two surgeons shaves the patient's hair, while the other places the woman's left arm under her body. The woman, however, weighs 118 pounds, so after a couple of minutes the anesthesiologist tries to position the arm in another way that is as comfortable for the woman as it is for the surgeons.

As the different excerpts show, patient positioning is the result of a series of negotiations and compromises. These may be more or less explicit but, in any case, they show how different professional visions concur in the processes of body manipulation and in achieving a correct positioning of the patient. 'Correctness' here refers to the fact that the positioning of a patient must reflect the needs of the different practitioners, taking into account both the type of surgery and the structure of the patient's own body. Annamarie Mol (2002) has notably argued that patients' bodies are not always the 'same body' in the eyes of different practitioners, and what we witness in these excerpts is precisely how in surgical practice different body reconstructions are aligned and made compatible with each other. In the three excerpts, patients' body becomes the main material reference for operators: its weight, its conformation, and the way it adapts to the technical objects it meets play a crucial role. Actors pay attention to how bodies "slide" on the operating table, the way a neck "stretches" on it, and to the kind of discomfort a position could cause to patients. Operators' professional vision leads them to focus on medical objects and bodies not as they were independent things, but as symbiotic elements of their practice. Because of this, sometimes practitioners compete to determine who has greater competence and/or legitimacy in deciding on the positioning of the patient, as in the following example:

Having positioned the patient on the operating bed, the instrument nurse asks the anesthesiologist: "Which is the ear to be operated on?" The anesthesiologist replies that it is the right one, and the instrument nurse retorts by saying: "Then the left arm should be positioned along the body, otherwise the doctor stands too far away." The anesthesiologist, however, would prefer to have the arm with the IV detached from the body so that she can check that the needle is in the vein. Thus, the IV is removed and inserted into the other arm. The instrument nurse concludes by saying: "However, it's a compromise, because both arms would go along the body. At [name of another hospital in the area] they do ear all day long and work like this... Anesthesiologist, I invite you to try it!"

In strictly organizational terms, the positioning of patients is the responsibility of the anesthesiologist, but here an instrument nurse intervenes claiming a different practice and expertise. Once again, what the actors discuss upon is how to position the body so that it is properly connected with the operating technologies (the IV, in this particular case) and thus with the surgical practice it will encounter. Indeed, it is worth noticing that the instrument nurse speaks in the name of the surgical practice (so to say), in that she argues about the far distance that would occur between the doctor and the patient's body, not about her own position or activity. As from the instrument nurse's reference to the hospital where *"they make ear all day and work like this"* the excerpt testifies the relevance of experience and material settings for actors' practices. This is even more apparent in the following episode:

The beginning of the operation is marked by the arrival of the Chief, who reminds the surgeon that an ophthalmologist is needed to remove a cyst from one patient's eye. The next day, the Chief asks the surgeon about the patient with the cyst on her eye: "Did the ophthalmologist remove it?". The Surgeon answers affirmatively and adds: "He wanted to be reassured, he wanted his instrument nurse, his instruments...and we kept telling him: "But what do you need?!?" [laughing]

The episode is indicative of how, as for scientists working in laboratories (Latour & Woolgar, 1979; Knorr-Cetina, 1981; Lynch, 1985), professional expertise is always linked to a context of action and objects in use. The ophthalmologist wants to work with the instrument nurse and with the instruments she already knows, demonstrating how feeling 'at ease' in the course of one's professional practice derives in large part from the affordances and the connections that a situated context offers and expresses in social and material terms.

6.3   Professional Vision and the Othertaking of Action

As underlined by ANT, we are never alone when we act, in that our action is accompanied by a series of material elements and other's people actions: most of the times, action is othertaken. In the above excerpt, what worries the ophthalmologist regards precisely what could happen once her action is othertaken by instruments and actors different from those involved in her daily activity. This same 'othertaking' of action is at the center of the next episode:

> In the course of a surgery, Luca (a newly hired anesthesiologist) gives Anna (nurse anesthetist) directions about the medication to inject the patient: "Give me 42cc of..."
> Anna: "42?!?"
> Luca: "Yes, 42, because the patient weighs 60 kilos." He pulls out of his pocket a notebook on which he has jotted down formulas and tables for dosing medication and shows it to Anna, to give her confirmation that the dosage is correct. Anna looks puzzled.
> When the procedure is completed, the patient is extubated and can be moved to the stretcher. The instrument nurse and Anna are now on the right side of the operating bed, while Luca is on the left. In an attempt to move the woman from the bed to the stretcher, Luca grabs the patient by the arm and pulls her toward him. Immediately Anna and the instrument nurse stop him: "No! Not like that! If you pull from the arm, you'll break it!". Luca smiles embarrassed.
> The stretcher on which the patient is standing is placed along the corridor separating the operating room from the pre-room, and when (about ten minutes later) Anna (from the operating room) sees that the patient is being taken away by the room staff nurse, she asks Luca: "Doctor, did you write down the parameters? I see you are sending the patient away....".
> Luca: "Ah, yeah... [turning to the room staff nurse who is carrying the stretcher] Sorry, just a moment, I forgot something...".
> Anna has a puzzled expression and during the next coffee break comments: "Asking to do 42cc with an insulin syringe is not normal. I told him yes, but I did 40, because you can't do 42!".

The episode is representative of those situations in which actors cannot take for granted the 'othertaking' of their action. The nurse anesthetist is worried by the practice of the new anesthesiologist, which does not correspond to her experience, nor to the materials present in the operating room. The request by the anesthesiologist to inject 42 cc of medication is indeed peculiar, in that insulin syringes present in the operating room could contain a maximum of 40 cc. Instruments, protocols, and their knowledge act as material demonstrations of operators' expertise, so that the new anesthesiologist appears as somebody who does not have confidence enough nor with the material infrastructure of surgical practice, nor with its organizational aspects (such as taking notes of some parameters before the patients leave the room). From this point of view, showing the notebook and stretching the patient from the arm further confirm to the nurse anesthetist the naïve professional vision of the anesthesiologist. It is probably on this basis that Anna decides to 'disobey' the anesthesiologist (administering a 40 cc dose to the patient instead of a 42 cc dose) and to follow with particular attention the moves of the colleague who, although with a higher professional status, nevertheless turns out to have a rough professional vision.

Having framed the symbiotic materialism and the way instruments are central to operators' professional visions (and to the encounter or conflict between different professional visions), in the next section, we will continue focusing on the sociomaterial dimension of different professional visions by taking into account some specific episodes in which actors are particularly concentrated on the encounters with and between different objects and events.

6.4   PROFESSIONAL VISION AS MATERIAL AWARENESS

Observations provide several instances of how operators carefully handle the interactions between various materials, as in the following case:

> Marilena just commented the afternoon was "quiet," when a nurse stops her along the corridor and announces the arrival of a "desectee" (a man with a ruptured aorta). There is only one cardiac surgery instrument nurse, but he is already engaged in another emergency, so Marilena has to instrument in the other room, even though she has never instrumented in that department before. "Let's hope for the best!", says Marilena as she quickly walks down the hallway to reach and talk to the head nurse. After having asked her which rooms are available, Marilena runs over room 8, reading on a sheet of paper what irons are needed and preparing them, along with the operating table.
>
> We leave Room 8 and head to the intensive care unit, where 118 personnel have just transported the patient. Here, around the patient, there are 8 operators. [...] The Chief of cardiac surgery also arrives and sits in front of

the PC and reads the result of the last test the patient underwent. Then he looks at Marilena and says to her: "You're there instrumenting, aren't you?!". Marilena replies yes, but immediately adds that she would rather replace the instrument nurse busy in the other cardiac surgery room and let the latter take care of the newly arrived patient. The Chief surgeon, trying to reassure her, replies: "Look, it's an easy one...," but Marilena does not seem convinced.

We leave resuscitation and head back to cardiac surgery. At the door, another instrument nurse whom Marilena meets tells her how complicated and delicate the surgery is on the patient who has just arrived. As Marilena enters the room, she tells to the instrument nurse engaged in the operation that she will replace him and that he will be in charge of the other case. She washes, gets dressed, and positions herself at the operating table, remarking to the two surgeons that she does not feel perfectly at ease instrumenting in this room. Smiling, the surgeons respond: "Don't worry, it's all quite simple." The fellow instrument nurse leaves the room and Marilena, apparently more serene, begins her work.

In this episode, what concerns the instrument nurse is not the emergency *per se*, but the organizational conditions it encounters (namely, the fact that there is already an emergency going on in one of the rooms) and her limited experience in instrumenting in the cardiac surgery room. In such a situation, the instrument nurse tries to rearrange the sociomaterial conditions of her action by negotiating with the other operators about her involvement, which allows her to 'swap' with a colleague and to take part in an emergency which has already been 'othertaken' by more experienced colleagues. Remarkably, the 'discomfort' the instrument nurse repeatedly expresses is compensated by the surgeons, who downplay the difficulty of the surgery and reassure her by apparently common sense expressions (*"it's an easy one," "it's all quite simple"*). As we have seen in occasion of the mimetic communication that often take place in the operating room, the meaning of such expressions is often embedded in the discursive practices of a particular organizational setting (see Chap. 4). In this case, by pointing to the 'easiness' and the 'simplicity' of the surgery, surgeons reframe its emergent nature and reconduct it to a kind of 'standard' professional knowledge that the instrument nurse surely possesses. From a certain point view, the instrument nurse's professional vision makes her aware of her limits, but surgeons' professional vision reassures her about her level of expertise.

In the opinion of all the actors encountered, colleagues are crucial to the development of a professional vision. According to the Head instrument nurse, for example, when there were fewer specialties "*you could see a little bit of everything,*" which meant that there was less fragmentation of knowledge, practices, and tricks of the trade. The Head nurse herself recalls how early in her career scrubs were made of fabric, so she was trained by her tutor to practice keeping her arms off her hips even for five or six hours, not to infect the scrub with her armpit sweat. With this short story, the Head nurse further testifies how bodies, work practices, and medical devices are intertwined, and thus the 'material awareness' that her professional practice and vision implies.

This material awareness is also what allows actors to improvise and solve unexpected situations during their work. In another informal conversation, the most senior nurse explained to the researcher that when there is an emergency (or an unforeseen event that substantially varies the operation being performed), you may not have the right needles and/or gauze and, in any case, probably there will be no time to count them. In these cases, the nurse says: "*maybe you ask the surgeon to check at the end, or you just count the smaller needles, which are the ones you're most concerned about... or, afterwards, you take an x-ray of the patient... You have to adapt a bit!*".

As we have seen in occasion of the 'flirts' actors have with the materials accompanying their work practices, operators are used to go beyond the script of different objects and technologies and read their multiple affordances (see Chap. 3). Here, we can witness how this process relates also to their professional vision and the material awareness it encapsulates. In the case just seen, for example, this material awareness translates in discerning between different objects on the basis of the probability they could be left into the patient's body, the consequences this could cause to the patient, and the possibility to check and solve later on an eventual problem.

6.5   Professional Vision and Sensemaking Processes

Perhaps because of the 'pragmatic' approach that practitioners (especially the more experienced ones) have developed toward work practices, an outsider may be impressed by the *nonchalance* with which they approach different technical objects. The loss of a needle during a procedure (for example) is an event that can easily cause hilarity among those in the room, and the gauze count can become an occasion for jokes, as from the following excerpt:

> The instrument nurse tells the surgeon 'closing' the patient to wait for the gauze count, but the surgeon replies: "There is definitely no gauze here." However, counts do not add up, and apparently one gauze is missing. The instrument nurse and nurse anesthetist begin searching the bins, while the room assistant nurse counts again. The anesthesiologist looks on the floor, the instrument nurse also looks in the bin where the doctors threw the scrubs (to see if there is gauze in the pockets), but they do not find anything. "Whatever, let's call radiology," the instrument nurse says.
>
> Suddenly, the surgeon says: "Excuse me, how much gauze did we use? Twenty, maybe twenty-five? Are we capable of losing one gauze when we use such a few?" After completing the sentence, he shows the gauze, slipping it off the patient's abdomen.

In this episode, the fact that operators ironize about their competence and the risks associated with surgical activity is indicative of the familiarity they have with the most common problems that can occur in the course of daily work. Counting gauze is a routine activity, and as for all routinized activities (or "Standard operating procedures," as Strauss and colleagues named them—Strauss et al., 1985), actors perfectly know how to handle them besides the exceptions or the misalignments that may happen. Studying how problematic situations are solved, Jordan (1992, quoted in Suchman, 1997) has highlighted the relationship between routines and improvisation, proposing the concept of "typified sequence of action" to interpret how in everyday work group members are oriented toward absorbing into the horizon of "a normal course of events" unexpected situations. So-called routines are indeed dependent on their faithful reproduction through competent practices: their reproduction is not ensured from the outside, but by those who put them into practice. As from ethnomethodology, routines constitute local outcomes in each case, so that the question regards precisely "the range of contingencies that can manifest themselves at different moments of activity (...) and how a sense of routine is reproduced" (Schegloff, 1986). Far from being tasks that form a program of action, routines always wait to be performed for "another first time" (Garfinkel, 1967: 9).

As seen, a misalignment in the gauze counting is such a common occasion that operators are plenty of possible solutions (asking the surgeon to check again, searching all around in the room, taking an x-ray of the patient), and they immediately relocate it in "a normal course of events" by making fun of the situation. In fact, in addition to particularly delicate surgical steps (such as intubating and extubating), what stimulates most the attention of experienced operators are situations in which a set of elements do not match, as in the case to follow:

> The anesthesiologist says that the upcoming surgery is quite risky, because it is performed within the rooms of the gastroenterology department, which are not adequately equipped for anesthesia, nor in case of an emergency. For this reason, she asks a fellow anesthesiologist (with whom she had spoken shortly before) to follow her into the room and to assist her.
> Together with the instrument nurse (who carries the anesthesia cart), the two anesthesiologists reach the ward. We meet the gastroenterologist who will perform the surgery and who has requested the anesthesiologist's assistance. The anesthesiologist asks him if there is a ventilator in Room1 (the room where the operation will take place), but the doctor replies in the negative. The two anesthesiologists then ask for the room to be changed and the patient be operated in Room4, the only one where there is a ventilator. After s short discussion, it is decided not to move the patient and instead to make room in Room1 for the ventilator.
> The two anesthesiologists read the patient's medical records and see that the most recent blood tests are four days old, and that the man is a former drug addict, taking methadone and suffering from cirrhosis and hepatitis C. The greatest concern of the two anesthesiologists, however, concerns the possibility of the man bleeding excessively during and after surgery. In fact, the patient has undergone this type of surgery before and on the previous occasion he remained in the intensive care unit for three days because of bleeding.

In this episode, as in so many other situations judged "dangerous" or "risky" by the operators, practitioners engage in complex evaluations, based on the exercise of technical knowledge as of a professional vision. As from the excerpt, this exercise permits the two anesthesiologists to engage in a process of sensemaking (Weick, 1995; Weick et al., 2005): they introduce order into the flow of events by noticing and isolating single elements (the ventilator, the blood tests, the clinical history of the patient); then they start labeling events employing a retrospective rationality (as for the "bleeding" of the patient); they continue to make sense of the situation by figuring out possible scenarios arising as result of medical action (as for the excessive bleeding of the patient during and after the surgery);

and they organize by communication (discussing about the situation and negotiating with the gastroenterologists to have the ventilator in the room).

To my knowledge, the relationship between professional vision and sensemaking processes has scarcely been investigated, except from a few studies in the field of education (Colestock & Sherin, 2009; McCausland et al., 2022). The episode just seen, by the way, clearly indicates how professional vision parallels sensemaking. The anesthesiologists' professional vision reinforces their sensemaking process, "creating opportunities to 'get somewhere' in relation to dilemmas they have" (McCausland et al., 2022). Sensemaking and professional vision emerge as ongoing processes that have no endpoint and that recursively interpellate each other.

From a sociomaterial point of view, we can notice how different elements participate to both these processes: actors, technologies, discussions, drugs, medical records, pathologies, and previous events. Some of these have a greater degree of sociality (as for actors or discussions), while others of materiality (as for technologies or drugs) but they are never 'pure' (as for medical records, pathologies, and previous events, which could be hardly classified in exclusively social or material terms). Sensemaking can thus be seen as more than an individual and collective process of organizing (Weick, 1995), but as a sociomaterial practice grounded in the negotiations between different professional vision and in the arrangement of various elements through communication.

6.6   Organizational Power as Sociomaterial Choreography

Together with professional visions, power asymmetries and hierarchies are at play at inter- and intra-professional levels. Examples of how these power asymmetries are reflected in communicative practices have already been given in the section about the way gender stereotypes are perpetuated at the organizational level. Now, we will see how asymmetries of power and status among different professions influence the way different practitioners relate to their work.

One should bear in mind that an operating team is by definition made up of actors with different levels of expertise: the first and second surgeons usually have different seniority, the instrument nurses may be more or less familiar with different types of surgery, between the anesthesiologist and nurse anesthetist, there may be an asymmetry in terms of expert knowledge, but also in terms of professional practice. Finally, room assistant nurses contribute to the surgery with a level of involvement that also inevitably varies depending on their knowledge of different clinical and work processes. This is to say that it is possible for hierarchies and rivalries to be in action at the same time at inter- and intra-professional levels, as in the many cases we have seen where there is disagreement between surgeons and instrument nurses, or when the first surgeon is dissatisfied with the work of the second.

Surgeons and anesthesiologists represent the two professional categories within the operating room who enjoy the higher status and autonomy. Professional status and power asymmetries are longstanding themes in the study of healthcare settings (Goffman, 1961; Foucault, 1963; Freidson, 1970), but my main interest here is to highlight their consequences from a sociomaterial point of view.

As seen in reference to the use of individual safety devices (see Chap. 3), the professional autonomy of these figures often results in a superior attitude toward organizational rules and safety protocols:

> Around 12 noon, the Head Nurse is used to make a tour of the different operating rooms. The moment we enter Cardiac Surgery, the anesthesiologist, not wearing mask nor gloves and talking on a cell phone, exits the room. I try to comment with the Head Nurse, who first reacts in the terms of: "Well, but he's the anesthesiologist..." [as if to say that he is not the one who is constantly in direct contact with the patient], and then adds: "It was already difficult to teach him not to keep the same pair of gloves throughout the day."

In this episode, what is perhaps most striking is not even the *nonchalance* with which the anesthesiologists relate to organizational safety rules and guidelines, but the impunity he enjoys. In the context observed, this impunity made it 'normal' for surgeons and anesthesiologists to adopt a rather discretional style toward safety prescriptions as a demonstration of their professional status. As from the answer given by an anesthesiologist to a surgeon who pointed out to him the dirtiness of his gown and mask: *"The day they tell the Chief that in the room like this you can't enter the room, I'll even put on a cap!"* (referring to the fact that the Chief surgeon was used to enter the operating room not properly dressed).

Moreover, if hierarchies and professional status are usually explicit, there is a further degree of variability related to the relationships among the organizational actors involved and to the relational attitudes of those actors, as from the following ethnographic excerpt:

> Lucio (instrument nurse) comments with one of his colleagues the unpolite attitude of a surgeon and how difficult it is working with him. Lucio confesses to his colleague that he asked the Head Nurse not to instrument for a while in this room, because "[the surgeon] looks at me as if I were an alien." The colleague replies: "And does he call you differently sometimes?" Lucio: "Yes! He calls me Fabio, Yuri, Giovanni...".

The episode testifies how surgeons may act their status not only by a discretionary attitude toward nonhumans (namely, personal protective equipment) but also toward humans, for example, by naming them casually, as if their individual subjectivity was purely accessory.

To favor the development of a common practice and attitude, the Head nurse has encouraged and supported the formation of somewhat cohesive groups, although this has sometimes led to the formation of conflicting subgroups. In the course of an informal conversation, the Head Nurse narrated that there are operators who cannot stand each other, "*and this, with 70 nurses, is just normal.*" The problem is, however, that some operators have started to spite each other. The Head Nurse, for example, told of operators openly stating in meetings that they hide irons and/or do not prepare the room appropriately when working with anesthesiologists or surgeons they do not go well along.

A certain amount of conflict is inherent in any group and organization, just as professional identity takes shape also in opposition to other identities and professions (as any other form of identity). In turn, power is a contested concept in organization studies (Hatch & Cunliffe, 2013), an unconcluded and never fully linear exercise, opening the door to both authority and resistance (Clegg, 2009). As noted by Fleming and Spicer (2014), power emerges through multiple 'faces' in and around organizations: it may imply coercion (when it forces to change behavior); manipulation (if it prevents the happening of certain occasions); domination (so to influence preferences); and subjectification (when it transforms individuals into subjects).

What we witness here, however, is how actors act the power connected to their professional status by means of a sociomaterial choreography. If the idea of choreography typically refers to a synchronized sequence of actions, in STS, it attains another quality, namely, the possibility to hold together divergent elements (Whalen et al., 2002; Michael, 2015), things that "can co-exist in sometimes uneasy way" (Watson et al., 2021: 1217). Charis Cussins (1996: 604), in particular, introduced this term to draw attention on how "materiality, structural constraint, performativity, discipline, co-dependence of setting and performers, and movement" are to be aligned in order to practice a routine.

Anesthesiologists or surgeons not properly wearing individual safety devices, for example, demonstrate their power by producing a sociomaterial choreography in which professionals and devices are not synchronized in the way prescribed by safety protocols and organizational rules. In the same vein, operators hiding irons or not preparing the operating room appropriately show their power by setting up a sociomaterial choreography aimed at disturbing anesthesiologists or surgeons' work. Finally, calling operators by different and wrong names can be taken as another demonstration of the ways in which it is possible to marginalize and 'downgrade' the actors involved in a sociomaterial choreography.

In all these occasions, power becomes a matter of performance and its choreography resides precisely in putting together contrasting elements: responsible operators (such as surgeons and anesthesiologists) not responsibly equipped, and/or participants to the scene not recognized in their role of actors. To stress the sociomaterial side of organizational power is thus a way to underline how different materials are mobilized when actors want to affirm their professional and hierarchical power. Object and other material device are mobilized to testify precisely how far the action of some professionals can go, and thus the power they have in transcending boundaries, norms, and sometimes people themselves.

REFERENCES

Clegg, S. R. (2009). Managing Power in Organizations: The Hidden History of its Constitution. In S. R. Clegg & M. Haugaard (Eds.), *The SAGE Handbook of Power*. Sage.

Colestock, A., & Sherin, M. G. (2009). Teachers' Sense-Making Strategies While Watching Video of Mathematics Instruction. *Journal of Technology and Teacher Education, 17*(1), 1059–7069.

Cussins, C. M. (1996). Ontological Choreography: Agency through Objectification in Infertility Clinics. *Social Studies of Science, 26*(3), 575–610.

Fleming, P., & Spicer, A. (2014). Power in Management and Organization Science. *The Academy of Management Annals, 8*(1), 237–298.

Foucault, M. (1963). *Naissance de la clinique*. PUF. [*The Birth of the Clinic: An Archaeology of Medical Perception*. London: Routledge, 1973].

Freidson, E. (1970). *Professional Dominance: The Social Structure of Medical Care*. Aldine.

Garfinkel, H. (1967). *Studies in Ethnomethodology*. Prentice Hall.

Goffman, E. (1961). *Asylums: Essays on the Social Situation of Mental Patients and Other Inmates*. Doubleday.

Goodwin, C. (1994). Professional Vision. *American Anthropologist, 3*, 606–633.

Goodwin, C. (2003). The Body in Action. In J. Coupland & R. Gwyn (Eds.), *Discourse, the Body and Identity* (pp. 19–42). Palgrave Macmillan.

Hatch, M. J., & Cunliffe, A. L. (2013). *Organization Theory: Modern, Symbolic, and Postmodern Perspectives*. Oxford University Press.

Knorr-Cetina, K. (1981). *The Manufacture of Knowledge. An Essay on the Constructivist and Contextual Nature of Science*. Pergamon Press.

Latour, B. (2005). *Reassembling the Social. An Introduction to Actor-Network Theory*. Oxford University Press.

Latour, B., & Woolgar, S. (1979). *Laboratory Life: The Social Construction of Scientific Facts*. Sage.

Lynch, M. (1985). *Art and Artifact in Laboratory Science: A Study of Shop Work and Shop Talk in a Research Laboratory*. Routledge and Kegan Paul.

McCausland, J., Jackson, J., McDonald, S., Bateman, K., Pallant, A., & Hee-Sun, L. (2022). Science Teachers' Negotiation of Professional Vision around Dilemmas of Science Teaching in Professional Development Context. *Journal of Science Teacher Education*.

Michael, M. (2015). Ignorance and the Epistemic Choreography of Method. In *Routledge International Handbook of Ignorance Studies* (pp. 84–91). Routledge.

Mol, A. (2002). *The Body Multiple: Ontology in Medical Practice*. Duke University Press.

Schegloff, E. A. (1986). The Routine as Achievement. *Human Studies, 9*, 111–151.

Strauss, A., Fagerhaugh, S., Suczek, B., & Wiener, C. (1985). *The Social Organization of Medical Work*. University of Chicago Press.

Suchman, L. (1997). Centers of Coordination: A Case and Some Themes. In L. Resnik, C. Saljo, C. Pontecorvo, & B. Burge (Eds.), *Discourse, Tools and Reasoning. Essays on Situated Cognition*. Springer Verlag.

Watson, A., Lupton, D., & Michael, M. (2021). The COVID Digital Home Assemblage: Transforming the Home into a Work Space During the Crisis. *Convergence, 27*(5), 1207–1221.

Weick, K. E. (1995). *Sensemaking in Organizations*. SAGE.

Weick, K., Sutcliffe, K., & Obstfeld, D. (2005). Organizing and the Process of Sensemaking. *Organization Science, 16*(4), 409–421.

Whalen, J., Whalen, M., & Henderson, K. (2002). Improvisational Choreography in Teleservice Work. *British Journal of Sociology, 53*, 239–258.

CHAPTER 7

Conclusions

Abstract This final chapter acknowledges the complexity and fluidity of the entanglements of objects, technologies, and actors. It discusses how objects and technologies initiate and organize events, monitor progress, affect orientation, and build collaborative action. Moreover, it stresses the gendered dimension of communicative practices and how power can be expressed by means of a sociomaterial choreography. Finally, it calls for a performative and sociomaterial approach to ethnography, while encouraging researchers to account for the empirical and theoretical contribution of their research.

Keywords Sociomaterial entanglements • Communicative practices • Sociomaterial choreography • Ethnographic accountability

> *"If social scientists do not understand people's definition of a situation, they do not understand it at all. (…) It makes no comment on where the definition of the situation may come from—human or nonhuman, structure or process, group or individual. It powerfully draws attention to the fact that the materiality of anything (action, idea, definition, hammer, gun, or school grade) is drawn from the consequences of its situation." (Bowker and Star, 1999: 289–290)*

121

In a paper I read just before writing these Conclusions, the authors state that after six years of ethnography it is hard to draw some clear conclusions. While sympathetic with the idea that ethnographies raise more questions than answers and having to struggle with myself every time I come to the concluding section of a paper or a book, I share authors' view. At the same time, I am convinced ethnographers should struggle with themselves in order to offer a comprehensive *albeit* situated interpretation of the reality they entered in. In this concluding section, thus, I will first schematically recall the main ways in which the continuous intertwining of objects, technologies, practices, and actors emerges at the organizational level and in the course of everyday work. Then, I will turn to the different "matters" of which communicative practices are made of: technical objects, but also bodies and gender. Lastly, I will quickly recall how objects and technologies play an equal central role in the making of professional expertise and in the choreography of organizational power. As already mentioned in the theoretical section (see Chap. 1), in each of these cases, the social and the material are not necessarily balanced in terms of degrees (Cooren, 2020), but they imply each other anyhow, at least partially.

Drawing on Nevile et al. (2014), it can be said that objects and technologies emerge in relation to different processes, such as:

- *initiating and organizing events and courses of action*—in organizational terms, the beginning of a surgery is marked by a telephone call; the operating list is essential for the actors knowing the order of patients and the surgery to be performed; the order on the list can be changed so to perform one after other surgeries which require the same instruments or the same positioning of the operating table; if surgical instruments are not "ready," the surgery cannot take place; before entering the operating room, operators have to wear personal protective equipment. These are probably the most striking examples of how objects and technologies come into play in the everyday organization of work and of their constitutive role for organizational practices in the operating room;
- *monitoring changing circumstances and attending to the progress of activities*—in the course of a surgery, various technologies are needed to monitor the patient's conditions; in case the body of a patient moves, further drugs have to be administered; the articulation of a surgery implies the movement and alternation of various objects and

technologies (such as scalpel at the beginning, the stitches at the end, and the lamp in the course of it); while the surgery proceeds, the room staff nurse constantly checks the number of gauzes that have been used. The progress of activities is thus the result of the alignment between human and technological action, in a reciprocal relationship where none of the two prevail on the other;

– *affecting orientation or change within the organizational environment*—when an object or a technology changes, breaks down, or is missing, actors need to reconfigure the situation, usually looking for the affordances other objects, technologies, architectures, and other materials at hand could offer; if the "gauze count" does not match at the end of a surgery, the surgeon stops closing the surgical field; in case the surgical field has already been closed but gauzes are missing, the patient may take an X-ray. These are just a few examples of the ways in which objects and technologies may attract actors' attention, shift routines, and reorient actors' practices;

– *building collaborative action and sensemaking*—at the beginning of the day, actors look for the operating list in order to figure out what kind of day will it be; actors refer and reconsider clinical records and/or previous exams in case of doubts or ambiguities; instrument nurses closely follow the order of the surgeries in order to have the necessary instruments sterilized at the right time; the presence of a particular technology or instrument is telling regarding the involvement of the different participants and the difficulty of the surgery itself. The presence, the knowledge, the use, and the sharing of technical objects thus call for collective action and sensemaking, while helping actors in framing the flow of the daily work. Communication and communicative practices play a central role in this process, being the means through which intersubjective interpretation and sensemaking happen;

– *realizing or facilitating particular forms of participation and involvement:* in the operating room, various sounds coming from different machines surround everyday activities, signaling to actors moments of emergencies and thus stimulating the action of specific practitioners; the radio or the music accompany the performance of the surgical procedures and help operators to concentrate and relax at the same time; the discussions that typically arise between different practitioners in relation to the positioning of the patient and the operating table are *de facto* occasions for the surgical équipe to negotiate and find agreements regarding the performance of the surgery. In all these cases, objects and technologies act as participatory devices, enabling and stimulating collective involvement through communication and aesthetic knowledge;

– *supporting thinking, perception, and learning:* the use of instruments and other technical objects represents a relevant portion of the training process of all the different professionals involved in a surgical team; patient's clinical record and/or previous exams can be crucial references to solve ambiguous situations; the explanation of an activity to a newcomer always includes the illustration of the technical objects implied by its performance, and often takes place through the use of such objects. These more than common situations remind the constitutive role objects and technologies have for surgical practice, stressing their continuous presence in learning and decision-making processes;

– *enhancing actors' mobility:* surgeons are equipped with a beeper in order to be quickly reached; smartphones are the technology implied for just-in-time communication; various phones in the operating block and in the surgical ward allow operators to communicate and look for each other; every morning, the instrument Head nurse uses her cell phone to contact staff who had not yet arrived, verify the availability of the personnel in order to substitute absentees, and be easily reachable by staff in emergency. Even if events took place in 2010 and thus in a not-yet digital world, information and communication technologies have already been incorporated in everyday work and everyday life, and they allow communication and coordination not only at distance, but while moving and continuing performing other tasks;

– *demonstrating and claiming knowledge:* mastering the use of technical objects is an integral part of a professional vision and a concrete demonstration of expertise; anticipating the technical requests of surgeons (the instrument to be used, the position of the lamp) is a crucial competence for instrument nurses and room staff nurses; if surgeons get nervous and/or they want to put pressure on their colleagues, they frequently complain because of the presence, the absence, or the positioning of a technical object; in conversations or controversies between surgeons and anesthesiologists, objects and technologies are frequently used as objective demonstrations of professional competence. In other words, technical objects are mobilized by actors in occasions they want to assert their professional knowledge and status, thus underlining the distance from other professional communities and other kinds of knowledge;

- *experiencing and acting upon the human body*: surgical instruments, anesthetic drugs, monitors, and a complex technical infrastructure and equipment are the means through which surgeons and anesthesiologists can attend to patients' bodies; nurse anesthetists need to insert a drip into the patient's arm in order to understand her/his pain perception; when acting upon bodies by means of instruments, actors experience also their own body, so that in neurosurgery (where smaller instruments and surgeries are made of slow and micro-movements), surgeons ask to operate barefoot in order to better balance the body and keep their hands steady. Through the use of objects and technologies, also the materiality of bodies emerges every time bodies and technologies do not 'fit' or properly 'react' to each other (as for the movements of the patients' body, even if anesthetized). From this point of view, objects and technologies do not mediate the experience operators have of the human body, but quite the opposite, in that they perform the body.

In other words, the sociomateriality of work in the operating room emerges through the constant orientation of actor's practices to the use, manipulation, incorporation, and sensemaking of a variety of objects and technologies. As seen through the previous tentative list of the ways in which objects and technologies shape work practices, artifacts may be implied in various processes and for various ends. Indeed, an opposite list could be made, addressing how objects and technologies may appear for:

- stopping and interfering with courses of action;
- detaching actors from their activity;
- maintaining the *status quo* in the organizational environment;
- obstructing collaborative action and understanding;
- complicating participation and involvement;
- misleading thinking, perception, and learning;

- forcing actors to stick to some places;
- demonstrating provisional knowledge;
- keeping a distance from the patients' bodies.

Instead of quickly recalling examples of these processes as in the previous list, I assume readers will be able to figure them out by themselves on the basis of the various episodes narrated throughout the previous chapters. In my interpretation, what is of interest is precisely that objects and technologies may have different uses, meanings, and ends depending on their function, form, and matter (Kallinikos, 2012), on the way they are practiced, on the relations they are part of, and on the actors and the other materialities they meet and have to be aligned with. "Objects are more or less viscous, and have different rhythms depending on where and when they are situated in networks" (Star, 1991: 277).

The two lists I just proposed, thus, have not to be interpreted in terms of the "effects" objects and technologies may have on organizational and work practices, but as the opposite sides of a *continuum* of effects arising from the entanglements of social and material practices. Table 7.1 presents an overview of such *continuum* of effects. Highlighting the variability in the outcomes resulting from the entanglements of the social and the material is crucial. This serves as a reminder that asserting the inherent

Table 7.1   Opposite sides of the *continuum* of effects arising from sociomaterial entanglements in the operating room

Initiating and organizing events and courses of action	Stopping and interfering with courses of action
Monitoring changing circumstances and attending to the progress of activities	Detaching actors from their activity
Affecting orientation or change within the organizational environment	Maintaining the status quo in the organizational environment
Building collaborative action and sensemaking	Obstructing collaborative action and understanding
Realizing or facilitating particular forms of participation and involvement	Complicating participation and involvement
Supporting thinking, perception and learning	Misleading thinking, perception and learning
Enhancing actors' mobility	Forcing actors to stick to some places
Demonstrating and claiming knowledge	Demonstrating provisional knowledge
Experiencing and acting upon the human body	Keeping a distance from the human body

sociomateriality of practices does not provide insights into the implications this interconnectedness may have for organizational and work processes. In short, while the social and the material are always entangled, the degrees and the outcomes of such entanglement may be different. Stating the sociomaterial entanglement of practices does not prevent from looking into the entanglement itself and from questioning its practical consequences.

As I have argued in Chap. 3, objects and technologies constitute the material infrastructure of everyday work and organizing practices and, from this point of view, they structure and stabilize actors' practices (Barley, 1986). As for any infrastructure (Star, 1999), objects and technologies shape and are shaped by the conventions of practices (as for the use of personal protective equipment); they are a *sine qua non* of membership in a community of professionals (as for the competence instrument nurses have in handling and monitoring different instruments); they do not have to be reinvented or reassembled each time (to each typology of surgery corresponds a stable set of instruments and technologies); and they embed standards and norms (as for safety standards). Tools and technologies thus become a natural part of the sociomaterial configuration of work practice. However, anomalies and breakdowns may happen, also considering the intrinsic complexity of a surgery and the density of objects, technologies, knowledges, and sociomaterial relations it implies. Focusing on situations where a technical artifact changes, breaks, or is absent, I have tried to underline an intrinsic characteristic of work and organizing practices in the operating room: the "flirting" with the material world.

Conceptualizing sociomaterial relations as a form of "flirtation" encompasses the tangible outcomes that arise from dynamic interactions between actors, objects, and technologies. These interactions can span from fleeting to enduring engagements, exhibiting varying levels of uncertainty and indeterminacy. The intimate relationship that develops between actors and instruments unifies various ethnographic episodes and is strengthened by the actors' continuous search for material elements that can serve as additional resources for action. Work goes beyond intentional performance and requires workers to be attentive to the possibilities for action that shape the ongoing flow of practice. Similar to a laboratory (Lynch, 1985), the operating room represents for practitioners not merely a collection of separate items but a meaningful whole that offers certain possibilities for action. When facing practical necessities, uncertainties, and urgencies, human subjects not only change their course of action, but also flirt with the material world in specific ways.

Furthermore, the metaphor of flirtation draws attention to the reciprocal bond that arises between actors and technological artifacts, highlighting the aesthetic ways in which actors become captivated by the material settings. A profound understanding, almost carnal, develops between the technical artifacts in the operating room and the bodies of the participants, compelling them to reflexively respond to the material prompts they encounter.

By the way, the sociomateriality of work and organizing practices in the operating room does not emerge only in relation to the complex technical apparatus which makes contemporary surgery possible, but also through language and communicative practices. As I have underlined in Chap. 4, communication in its multiple forms plays a prominent role in the operating room: from an organizational point of view, the beginning of a surgical session entails the use of a technology (the telephone), and together with it a series of face-to-face and remote interactions. Even though surgeries take place mostly in silence, silence should not be confused with any kind of absence (Rich, 1978, quoted in Star, 1991). Most of the communication has indeed mimetic characteristics, in that it is camouflaged with common sense expressions and/or short sentences. "Everything okay?", "Ready?", "The patient is moving!", or "The lamp!" are usually addressed to nobody in particular and imply entire and collective courses of action.

Objects and technologies participate to discourses for various reasons: they compose a good portion of the technical vocabulary used by organizational actors and often become matter of discussion, the most common example being the Head nurse frequently discussing with surgeons and anesthesiologists regarding the proper use of personal protection equipment. In particular, the main skill refers to how fast operators are in managing technical devices, so that I have underlined how through language technical artifacts become sorts of objective demonstrations of actors' skills and velocity.

I have also highlighted a parallel process, by which discourses become constitutive of objects. Indeed, the work performed by operators for a technology to properly function sometimes is a communicative work aimed at anticipating some of the features of the technical artifacts at stake. From a certain point of view, this pairing technology's presence and effects with words can be interpreted as part of the sentimental work (Strauss et al., 1985) nurses typically perform when administering drugs or therapeutic treatments. In other occasions by the way, communication is crucial in order to monitor how and/or what the patient feels. This is something technology itself cannot check, and this is why operators involve patients as active communicative agents of technology's action. Through communicative practices, organizational actors give voice to what technologies should or should not do, thus materializing parts of their effects, and keeping machines and bodies aligned.

Another side of the sociomaterial dimension of work and organizing practices emerges precisely in relation to bodies and the way they are gendered. Together with objects and technologies, communicative practices in the operating room perform also gender stereotypes and relations. In particular, they construct a virile masculinity which finds expression in (for example) the heroic dimension with which surgeons often speak of (and act out) the daily work; the cold and detached attitude that many anesthesiologists display in the course of operations; or the ancillary position that characterizes some professional figures (typically, the room staff nurse, the anesthesiologist nurse, and the instrument nurse). In this way, gender becomes another "matter" organizational, work, and communicative practices are made of. Within a community whose gender order relegates the feminine to a subaltern role, women have to manage the "hostess role" (Timmons & Tanner, 2005) frequently assigned to them. As from various ethnographic excerpts, in most of the cases, they simply do not reply to the "jokes," the "teasing," and the "attentions" male surgeons and anesthesiologists direct to them, thus positioning through silence out of the masculine perimeter. Although quite rare, moreover, women themselves may mobilize masculine communicative practices, either to detour them, either to pay homage to the emphasized femininity (Connell, 1995) aimed at confirming and satisfying the canons of masculine heroism and bravado.

The idea of gender as a "material-semiotic" arrangement is already present in Haraway's work (Haraway, 1991, 1997), and framing gender, the body, and the subject as results of a more or less stable network of sociomaterial practices does not constitute a novelty neither in OS nor in STS (Law, 1994; Bruni & Gherardi, 2001; Bruni et al., 2005; Fujimura, 2006; Perrotta, 2013; Franklin, 2013; Styhre & Arman, 2013). However, we witness here something slightly different. Namely, how gender can be conceived as the product of sociomaterial practices, but also as part of the "matter" sociomaterial practices are made of. Maybe the time has come to affirm that practices are sociomaterial and that gender is precisely one of the most common elements they are made of.

Taking into account the gender(ed) dimension of communicative practices, thus, also power dynamics emerge. In Chap. 5, in particular, I have shown how power can be exerted by means of a sociomaterial choreography. In STS, the concept of choreography refers to the ability to hold together the divergent elements required to execute a routine (Cussins, 1996). Anesthesiologists or surgeons not properly wearing their personal protective equipment and/or operators failing to adequately prepare the operating room both assert their power by creating a sociomaterial choreography in which professionals and devices deviate from the prescribed safety protocols and organizational rules. Thus, power becomes a performance, whose choreography lies in an arbitrary alignment of movements, material artifacts, and actors.

As in every organizational setting, power relates to the different hierarchical and professional status actors occupy in the organizational structure: surgeons and anesthesiologists clearly occupy a leadership position, especially in relation to nurses. At the same time, power in organization manifests also in relation to the role and the competence actors display inside specific communities of practice. In particular, we have seen how in the observed context what specifies actors' professional vision is what I have defined as "symbiotic materialism" and "material awareness." The former refers to the ability most skilled actors have in paying attention to each other's action and simultaneously to the technical objects involved by that action. Strictly related to this idea, material awareness refers to taking into account the intertwinement of bodies, medical devices, and organizational and work practices. For example, to discern between different objects on the basis of the consequences they could cause to the patient's body, and of the remedial practices implied by an eventual problem.

Overall, a sociomaterial reading of organizational and work practices in the operating room returns a contrasting image, in which actors, objects, and technologies continuously othertake (Latour, 2005) each other's action. This contrasting image also applies to the organizational setting, whose main characteristics seem to revolve around a constant alternating of unpredictability and standard operating procedures. There can be diverse examples: from the head nurse who schedules a higher number of staff for each shift than theoretically necessary (knowing that there might easily be unexpected absences or delays); to the instrument nurses who bring with them more surgical instruments to the operating room than technically required (in order to accommodate the preferences of different surgeons and handle unforeseen incisions); to the anesthesiologists who equip themselves with additional medications as a buffer for particularly serious situations. It is thus not surprising that there are small but continuous unforeseen events to which actors respond without particular concern. This is part of the everyday work in the operating room, and in a sense, it testifies the confidence actors have developed in relation to organizational and work practices. A significant portion of the operators' daily work lies precisely in trying to ensure that as many details as possible (patients, surgeons, nurses, technical objects, protocols, etc.) are aligned, and to remedy immediately in case of missing elements or links. In this ongoing process, all the invisible work (Star & Strauss, 1999) carried out by organizational actors becomes manifested, and ethnographic accounts have sought to highlight it.

Discussing the challenges a sociomaterial approach poses to ethnography, I have sketched the importance of passing from a representational and constructivist view to a performative and sociomaterially entangled approach (see Chap. 2). This means approaching organizational processes looking for the connections among different courses of action, and to grasp how objects and subjects define each other in relations. From this point of view, shadowing sociomaterial processes requires the ethnographer to be able to orient his/her observations to the practices that perform relations, and probably also to devise new narrative forms able to make that performance accountable. I am not referring here to the need of a post-qualitative and nonrepresentationalist approaches to academic writing (Benozzo et al., 2019; Cozza, 2021), but to the possibility of finding an infralanguage (Latour, 2005) able to account for the role of objects and the study of "boring things" (Star, 1999). Boredom springs from the inertia of matter or from the monotonous repetition of the same actions: things (such as surgical instruments and technologies) may be boring perhaps because of the organizational relations in which they are involved, not because of their properties. Thus, an ethnographic approach may help to show that matter is not so 'inert' and that the monotonous repetition of actions is something that also pertains to ethnographic accounts. Recognizing the various types of action that give concrete form to organizational action may therefore be a route to follow when observing the sociality of objects and delving into the materiality of the social (Bruni, 2005).

According to Hess (2001), the quality of an ethnography should always be assessed in relation to the depth of knowledge the author demonstrates with respect to the object of study; the ability to contribute to a theoretical debate; and the presence of unexpected or counterintuitive data. Given these criteria, which from my point of view could apply to any social research, I gladly leave the final word to readers regarding the results of the present research and the theoretical contribution made by an ethnographic and sociomaterial approach to organizational and work practices in the operating room.

REFERENCES

Barley, S. R. (1986). Technology as an Occasion for Structuring: Evidence from Observations of CT Scanners and the Social Order of Radiology Departments. *Administrative Science Quarterly, 31*, 78–108.

Benozzo, A., Carey, N., Cozza, M., Elmenhorst, C., Fairchild, N., Koro-Ljungberg, M., & Taylor, C. A. (2019). Disturbing the Academic Conference Machine: Post-Qualitative Re-turnings. *Gender, Work and Organization, 26*, 87–106.

Bowker, G., & Star, S. L. (1999). *Sorting Things Out: Classification and its Consequences*. MIT Press.

Bruni, A. (2005). Shadowing Software and Clinical Records: On the Ethnography of Non-humans and Heterogeneous Contexts. *Organization, 12*(3), 357–378.

Bruni, A., & Gherardi, S. (2001). Omega's Story: The Heterogeneous Engineering of a Gendered Professional Self. In M. Dent & S. Whitehead (Eds.), *Managing Professional Identities: Knowledge, Performativity and the 'New' Professional*. Routledge.

Bruni, A., Gherardi, S., & Poggio, B. (2005). *Gender and Entrepreneurship. An Ethnographic Approach*. Routledge.

Connell, R. W. (1995). *Masculinities*. University of California Press.

Cooren, F. (2020). Beyond Entanglement: (Socio-) Materiality and Organization Studies. *Organization Theory, 1*, 1–24.

Cozza, M. (2021). Affective Engagement in Knowledgemaking. *Tecnoscienza. Italian Journal of Science & Technology Studies, 12*(2), 115–123.

Cussins, C. M. (1996). Ontological Choreography: Agency Through Objectification in Infertility Clinics. *Social Studies of Science, 26*(3), 575–610.

Franklin, S. (2013). *Biological Relatives. IVF, Stem Cells, and the Future of Kinship*. Duke University.

Fujimura, J. H. (2006). Sex Genes: A Critical Sociomaterial Approach to the Politics and Molecular Genetics of Sex Determination. *Signs, 32*(1), 49–82.

Haraway, D. (1991). *Simians, Cyborgs, and Women: The Reinvention of Nature*. Routledge.

Haraway, D. (1997). *Modest Witness @Second Millenium.FemaleMan Meets OncoMouseTM: Feminism and Technoscience*. Routledge.

Hess, D. (2001). Ethnography and the Development of Science and Technology Studies. In P. A. Atkinson, A. Coffey, S. Delamont, J. Lofland, & L. Lofland (Eds.), *Handbook of Ethnography* (pp. 234–245). Sage.

Kallinikos, J. (2012). Form, Function and Matter: Crossing the Border of Materiality. In P. M. Leonardi, B. A. Nardi, & J. Kallinikos (Eds.), *Materiality and Organizing: Social Interaction in a Technological World* (pp. 68–87). Oxford University Press.

Latour, B. (2005). *Reassembling the Social. An Introduction to Actor-Network Theory*. Oxford University Press.

Law, J. (1994). *Organizing Modernity*. Blackwell.

Lynch, M. (1985). *Art and Artifact in Laboratory Science: A Study of Shop Work and Shop Talk in a Research Laboratory*. Routledge and Kegan Paul.

Nevile, M., Haddington, P., Heieneman, T., & Rauniomaa, M. (2014). On the Interactional Ecology of Objects. In M. Nevile, P. Haddington, T. Heieneman, & M. Rauniomaa (Eds.), *Interacting with Objects* (pp. 3–31). John Benjamins Publishing Company.

Perrotta, M. (2013). Creating Human Life Itself. The Emerging Meanings of Reproductive Cells among Science, State and Religion. *Tecnoscienza: Italian Journal of Science & Technology Studies, 4*(1), 7–22.

Star, S. L. (1991). The Sociology of the Invisible: The Primacy of Work in the Writings of Anselm Strauss. In D. R. Maines (Ed.), *Social Organization and Social Process* (pp. 265–283). De Gruyter.

Star, S. L. (1999). The Ethnography of the Infrastructure. *American Behavioral Scientist, 43*, 377–391.

Star, S. L., & Strauss, A. (1999). Layers of Silence, Arenas of Voice: The Ecology of Visible and Invisible Work. *Computer-Supported Cooperative Work, 8*(1/2), 9–30.

Strauss, A., Fagerhaugh, S., Suczek, B., & Wiener, C. (1985). *The Social Organization of Medical Work*. University of Chicago Press.

Styhre, A., & Arman, R. (2013). *Reproductive Medicine and the Life Sciences in the Contemporary Economy. A Sociomaterial Perspective*. Gower.

Timmons, S., & Tanner, J. (2005). Operating Theatre Nurses: Emotional Labour and the Hostess Role. *International Journal of Nursing Practice, 11*(2), 85–91.

INDEX[1]

[1] Note: Page numbers followed by 'n' refer to notes.